The Art of Business Negotiation

THE ART OF BUSINESS NEGOTIATION

A Harvard Business Review Paperback

Harvard Business Review paperback No. 90027

ISBN 0-87584-288-7

The *Harvard Business Review* articles in this collection are
available as individual reprints, with the exception of "Do We
Really Want Labor on the Ropes?" and "The Case for Adversarial Unions." Discounts apply to quantity purchases. For information and ordering contact Operations Department,
Harvard Business School Publishing Division, Boston, MA
02163. Telephone: (617) 495-6192, 9 a.m. to 5 p.m. Eastern
Standard Time, Monday through Friday. Fax: (617) 495-6985,
24 hours a day.

Editor's Note: Some articles in this book may have been written before authors and editors began to take into consideration the role of women in management. We hope the archaic
usage representing all managers as male does not detract from
the usefulness of the collection.

Printed in the United States of America by Harvard
University, Office of the University Publisher.
93 92 91   5 4 3 2 1

Contents

Negotiation in the Global Marketplace

Staying Out of Court

Roger Fisher

He who pays the piper

A 'CEO' questions outside counsel about the pressures to litigate rather than settle cases and suggests ways that together they might change that pattern

Can a corporation avoid the quagmire of litigation? Are there ways to keep outside counsel under control? Is it possible to convert guns for hire into cost-effective dispute resolvers? Roger Fisher, an expert in negotiation and the nonlitigious settlement of disputes, describes what he would do if he were a corporate executive faced with skyrocketing legal bills from a blue-chip firm. He presents his thoughts in a hypothetical letter from a chief executive to a lawyer in a firm that handles major litigation for the company.

Mr. Fisher is Williston Professor of Law at Harvard University, director of the Harvard Negotiation Project, and the author (with William Ury) of Getting to YES: Negotiating Agreement Without Giving In *(Houghton Mifflin, 1981; Penguin, 1983). Before joining the Harvard Law School in 1958, he practiced law for a number of years. He is also senior consultant to Conflict Management, Inc., a small Cambridge, Massachusetts firm that specializes in negotiation and in dispute resolution.*

Illustration by John Devaney.

March 1, 1985

Mr. C. Ewen Cort
Litigation Department
Marshall, Holmes, Lincoln & Stone
Wall Street
New York, New York 10005

Dear Chuck:

As we get started on the new fiscal year, I thought we might jointly review the relationship between our company and your firm to see if it could be improved. I am sure that at times we have not been as helpful to you as we might have been. And on some occasions, particularly when we receive your monthly statements, I wonder if we are making the best use of the great talent found in your firm.

This is going to be a long letter, spelling out some of my concerns and advancing a few ideas for our joint consideration. Don't get worried: we are not planning to switch our major litigation business to some other firm (although negotiation theory suggests that we should always have our best alternative in mind). What I propose to do is to identify some symptoms, diagnose possible explanations, and advance some general approaches and specific remedies that we may want to think about together.

After you have had a chance to read this letter and to discuss it with some of your partners, I suggest that a few of us—perhaps two or three from your firm and two or three from my company—schedule half a day or more when we can talk about how we might work more effectively together. I am sure that jointly we can come up with better ideas than those I have produced alone.

What concerns us

One issue, of course, is the amount of money that we have devoted to paying legal fees, particularly for matters in pending or anticipated litigation. If you will review the total sum that we have paid your firm over the past several years for litigation, I am sure you will agree it is large. Some would call it staggering.

A second concern is the amount of our corporate executives' time that lawsuits consume. Interviews by lawyers, interrogatories, depositions, searches through the files for relevant documents, and attempts to recall just what was said when—all these take valuable time away from business. And it is not just a question of time. Litigation also entails stress, worry, and energy, all of which divert our attention from creative pursuits. Being in a fight is upsetting. Our emotions get caught up in a lawsuit. Preparing for deposition or cross-examination has a high human cost even if, as so often happens, the case is settled before trial.

From the point of view of the parties to a lawsuit, the costs are in vain; almost every litigated case is a mistake. If we and our adversary in a given lawsuit were smart enough (or well enough advised), we could settle the case together, even before it is filed, for roughly the same amount as the final judgment. We could avoid the agony and save the legal fees. And in many cases, if we had worked side by side with the other party, we could have agreed on a creative solution that served our interests far better than any judgment a court might order.

Sometimes, to be sure, we are interested in establishing a good precedent or avoiding a bad one. Experience suggests, however, that it is hard enough just to win a case, let alone do so in a way that will establish a desirable legal precedent. And a bad precedent is more likely to be set by a judicial opinion than by a unique settlement. Moreover, one large public judgment against us is far more likely to stir up additional litigation than a half-dozen quiet settlements.

My concerns come down to this: the costs of litigation are high; too many cases are litigated; and those that are settled tend to be settled late, less than optimally, and only after large amounts of time and money have been spent on depositions, document discovery, motions, and other pretrial measures. Why? What are some possible reasons for unduly expensive and time-consuming trials and late settlements?

Why we don't settle our cases

Employing foresight and wisdom, we and our litigation adversaries ought to settle most of our disputes at an early stage. Why don't we? Let me advance a number of hypotheses.

Litigious working assumptions

American business people suffer from a lawyer's perception of what constitutes the "normal" way to deal with a dispute. Lawsuits are often filed and answered without anyone even talking with the people on the other side. If we ask your firm's advice about a dispute that might end up in court, our query goes directly to the litigation department. As much as I approve of the efforts now being made in behalf of mediation, minitrials, and other forms of "alternative dispute resolution," I don't like that name. It reinforces the assumption that the normal way to deal with differences is to take them to court, and that to talk with the other side about settling a case is a new and unusual alternative to what lawyers regularly do.

Other assumptions, widely held by lawyers, tend to aggravate the pressure toward litigation. If I am correct, members of the litigation bar usually operate on the premise that it is a sign of weakness to be the first party to propose settlement talks. "If we suggest settlement," the thinking goes, "they will think we must have a poor case; their expectations will go up."

I have also heard lawyers say, "We can't talk settlement until discovery is completed." Others insist that until the case is fully prepared for trial, and until they know what judge is going to sit on the case, it is too early to contemplate settling. Even then, some are reluctant to favor settlement because "you just can't tell what a judge or jury will do." While such uncertainties may deter lawyers, we in business make decisions every day under conditions even more uncertain.

Another obstacle to settlement is the lawyer's rule that the most likely time to settle a case is just before trial "on the courthouse steps." With that norm in mind, lawyers tend to postpone all settlement discussion until the last minute.

You can probably provide us with an even more accurate and persuasive set of working hypotheses for why lawyers tend to prevent or postpone settlement.

Clients' distorted judgment

A number of factors tend to make both this corporation and your firm litigation prone. Let me first look at those that may cause us to litigate more often than is in our own best interest.

Emotions. In any dispute, a partisan becomes emotionally involved. We are likely to get angry. Our egos are on the line. We want to be vindicated. We do not want to be "taken." We do not want to be seen as backing down.

Passing the buck. To the corporate officer involved in a dispute, a recommendation to settle may suggest that he or she has made a mistake. (In one case that I know of, the "mistake" cost over $180 million. No corporate official wants to admit errors like that.) From the corporate officer's point of view, it looks better to refer the case to the lawyers, to outside counsel. If the case is lost, it is the fault of the lawyers, or of the judge or jury. And besides, the judgment will not be entered for years, by which time the corporate officer may well be in a different job.

Not only do officers feel the pressure to pass the buck but, in a large case, the board of directors itself also feels it. If the board approved a pricing policy or an action causing environmental pollution, members may much prefer to pass that issue on to the courts—even at great corporate expense—rather than settle a case from which others could infer that their judgment had been mistaken.

Conflicts of interest. In some instances there may be a clear conflict of interest between an officer and the corporation. The corporation pays the legal fees; if vindicated in court, the officer "wins." Suppose an officer is clearly responsible for a very profitable but controversial decision that is a central issue in a major dispute headed for court. Objectively, the company may have only a 30% chance of winning the case. At the same time, it has an opportunity to settle on terms that are fair and will avoid a large downside risk for the corporation. From the officer's point of view, it makes little difference whether the corporation pays a substantial amount now or a much larger amount later; both are bad and reflect poorly on the officer's judgment. But because a lawsuit just might, conceivably, vindicate the officer's judgment, it may be far better for the officer to have the corporation litigate. In any event, postponing the bad day, if bad it must be, is more attractive than paying up now.

Time is money. Perhaps the most important disincentive, especially when large amounts are at stake and when interest rates are high, is the value of money over time. A corporate defendant may know that, eventually, it will have to pay, say, $100 million. Because most claims do not accumulate prejudgment interest, every year's postponement of the evil day saves the interest on $100 million. Settling a big case in which we are the defendant may hurt this quarter's bottom line. Generally, whatever the amount involved in either a settlement or a court decision, financial managers would prefer to put off bad news. Other things being equal, a large negative line item will, if possible, always be put off to the next fiscal period.

Partisan bias. Whether any of the factors I have mentioned operate on a conscious or an unconscious level, a corporate officer is likely to take an unduly optimistic view of any controversy in which he or she is involved. Simply looking at a situation as a partisan tends to distort one's judgment. A professor has tested this notion by giving students identical facts about a hypothetical company that is for sale—balance sheets, cash flow, inventory, and so forth. One-half the students act as potential buyers of the company, and the other half as sellers. After they have prepared for negotiation, but before negotiations have begun, the professor asks each student to write out privately his or her best estimate of the price that an impartial arbitrator would set. Of the more than one thousand students who have engaged in this exercise, sellers routinely name a substantially higher figure than do buyers. Simply looking at the same information from a different point of view causes people to collect and emphasize the data that best support their interests.

I am sure that the longer we consider our side of a controversy, the more biased our judgment becomes. Certainly, we look at our side of a dispute more often than we do our opponent's side. It is only natural that we talk ourselves into believing ever more strongly in the justice of our cause. Such corporate overconfidence may help explain why so often we urge you to pursue litigation.

Lawyers' distorted judgment

Admitting that we clients may be more prone to litigate than we should be, it seems to me that you lawyers are subject to many, if not more, of the same weaknesses.

Emotions. Certainly some trial lawyers practice litigation because they love the contest. They find pleasure in representing a client with the full zeal that the legal canons of ethics call for. They like to engage in battle and they like to win. *Their* egos, too, are on the line. For some lawyers, negotiating the set-

tlement of a case being prepared for trial has about as much appeal as negotiating the settlement of a football game or a prizefight would have for the athletes. (For others, I am sure, a good settlement can feed the ego as much as any trial.)

Passing the buck. You lawyers are human, too. You must surely have a tendency to avoid taking responsibility for recommending either that the large claims sought in a court battle be settled for lesser amounts or that substantial sums be paid out in settlement of a claim that you are contending is worthless. (One lawyer told me that he felt a little silly having his client accept his recommendation for a settlement in one of the aluminum cases, and then seeing co-defendants, who did not settle, win their cases and get off scot-free.) If you win a case, it is a great victory for you. If you lose, you did your best; you can blame the defeat on the court or on the conduct of the corporation.

Conflicts of interest. Even when a firm's long-term interest in providing high-quality service at minimum cost might favor settling a case, the incentives for individual lawyers may pull in another direction. You expect your young associates to turn in a large number of billable hours. Indeed, in many firms today the more billable hours young lawyers turn in, the better their chances of making partner. Rarely, I daresay, are they thanked for being cost-conscious, for limiting the amount of time they spend on a case, and for going home early in the evening.

On the other hand, should those lawyers ever fail to find an obscure but relevant precedent – a needle in a haystack discovered by opposing counsel – they would run the risk of incurring serious criticism. Under these circumstances, young lawyers must feel pressure to keep the meter running.

Financial disincentives. From the point of view of your firm as a whole, the financial incentives to litigate a case or to settle at the last moment, rather than earlier, must be enormous. Just look again at the aggregate amount of the legal fees that your litigation department has earned working on our cases. Most of that high-priced time was spent on discovery, motions, trial preparation, trials, and appeals, not on negotiating settlements. You have high overhead costs and high salaries for your young lawyers, all of which you must pay before you partners can receive the large incomes that you have come to expect. A big case is to a law firm as a good milking cow is to a dairy farmer: a reliable source of steady income. I don't mean to be critical; I'm just stating facts.

Is this also true for lead trial counsel like yourself? One or two major law firms, I understand, divide annual profits equally among all partners. Most, I believe, apportion the firm's net income among the partners in ways that reflect time spent, new clients brought in, and revenue generated by the cases the partners have brought in or on which they worked. For example, would your personal income, and that of some of your colleagues in the litigation department, have been lower over the last couple of years if more of our company's cases had been settled at an early date? If so, is there any chance that personal financial consequences subconsciously affect your judgment about which cases we ought to settle and which we ought to litigate?

What is true for you may also, of course, to an even greater extent be true for opposing counsel. A solo practitioner may have only one big case – one milking cow. The possibility of settlement may loom as a major disaster. Another lawyer may be on a contingent fee and have time available. The possibility of a whopping fee, no matter how remote, may be far more attractive than a quick settlement in the client's interest.

I have heard of lawyers with a contingent-fee contract preventing a settlement the client wanted. A manufacturing company offered to settle a claim for defective products by providing the next year's supply of parts free. The lawyer was not the least bit interested in receiving one-third of such parts as his fee.

Partisan bias. At the start of a case, outside counsel are perhaps more pessimistic than optimistic. Because they try to avoid raising their client's expectations, they look at a case from the adversary's point of view. But the longer you lawyers work on one side of a case, the more likely you are to become convinced that that side ought to prevail.

Part of your effectiveness as an advocate depends on your first persuading yourself that your arguments are sound. Lawyers sometimes fail to persuade courts of their case's merits, but they rarely fail to persuade themselves. Even when they are far from certain that they will win, they tend, I believe, to overestimate the odds. A 50-50 case becomes a probable victory; a 20% chance of winning becomes a 50-50 case. Rather than help offset the client's bias, a lawyer's judgment may instead reinforce it.

Again, what is true for you will also be true for lawyers on the other side.

Role of counsel

These factors, which tend to operate against settlement and in favor of litigation, suggest that perhaps we should reexamine the role in which our current client-lawyer relationship places you. Too often, I fear, we both see your job as that of skilled advocates and guns for hire – soldiers we retain to do battle against our adversaries. As a corporate plaintiff, we see ourselves seeking justice from those who have violated our rights. As a corporate defendant, we see ourselves resisting outrageous suits stirred up by unscrupulous lawyers hoping for large contingent fees.

In either case, we see you as our knight in shining armor, ready (for a fee) to fight to the end in vindication of our cause. In the tradition of the military hero, off you go to fight the good fight, to overcome every obstacle, and to persevere to the end, whether it be bitter or sweet.

But maybe we need less of a brave Sir Galahad and more of a wise Merlin—someone to cool our partisan tempers and to remind us of the corporate interest in settling cases quickly, efficiently, and fairly. Maybe we have the wrong image of what we want you to do. In the end, most of our cases get settled rather than determined by the judgment of a court. If this is true, then perhaps, for starters, you should change the name of your part of the firm from the "litigation department" to the "settlement department" or the "negotiation department." Might such a change in nomenclature help us see your role in a different light?

Little work on settlement

It's fair to say, I believe, that although most lawsuits get settled, your time is still largely devoted to the alternative means of resolving differences, namely litigation. Our judgment on whether to settle or litigate may suffer from the disproportionate amount of time that you spend on the litigation option. Together we spend a great deal of time trying to prove the worst case about our adversary's past conduct but little time trying to structure a future arrangement that would be to our mutual advantage.

You develop a litigation strategy but no settlement strategy. You think at length about the best questions to ask during cross-examination but you rarely devise the best questions to ask in negotiating a settlement. You have a clear idea of the most we should ask for in damages but you have little notion of the least we should accept in settlement. You formulate clear arguments for why, when we are the defendant, we owe nothing, but you arrive at no clear figure for the maximum amount we should be prepared to pay in settlement.

We corporate clients are probably even worse when it comes to thinking about settlement. Once we have given a case to outside counsel, we are likely to see it as "their problem."

Can we change our practice?

These diagnoses point to some remedies that we should explore.

Foster a new working assumption

Could we introduce into your way of doing business and ours the premise that it is in the interest of all parties to settle every case promptly and fairly? Litigation should be a last resort: it is better than dueling but much more expensive. As soon as you could prepare yourselves to do so, you might initiate settlement talks with the other side—not because your case is weak but because your client has given you standing instructions to that effect.

Nor should you postpone settlement talks until you have gathered all possible evidence and removed all possible uncertainties. Even with the best of discovery, litigation is always uncertain. Gathering data may well not be worth either the cost or the time. Furthermore, uncertainty may promote settlement. Depending on the parties' aversion to risk, a modest and quick payment to resolve a dispute in which neither side has invested much may be an ideal outcome for both. Like an insurance premium, it may be a small price to pay to avoid uncertainty. And when we are the plaintiff, particularly when we are business people whose time is probably best spent in other ways, a bird in the hand may be worth quite a few in the bush.

Presumably, if we clients make our wishes clear, you lawyers can pursue our interests in settlement with all the zeal that you now devote to litigation. What general guidance could we propose, what working assumptions might be most useful, to switch outside counsel's pattern of behavior away from litigation and toward the prompt settlement of disputes?

An advocate for settlement?

To improve the quality of judicial decisions, you lawyers rely on the adversary process. You have convinced yourselves—and most of us—that it is difficult for a judge to decide wisely without hearing both sides. No lawyer is expected to argue the case for both sides. The chance of the judge's reaching a sound decision is enhanced by having different people present the cases for different courses of action.

Because we end up litigating more often than we should, I fear that as a client I am making poor decisions. Perhaps I, like a judge, would benefit from the adversary process. Perhaps we, as a corporation, would reach wiser decisions if we had one lawyer develop the case for litigation and a different lawyer press on us the case for settlement. Wouldn't that be a logical application of the adversary process to which you are so deeply committed?

There seems no feasible way to avoid emotional involvement, partisan bias, and the natural desire to pass the buck. If we have to live with these risks, shouldn't we create a countervailing force that will give us the opposing case clearly and persuasively? If a judge needs opposing advocates to produce a good decision, perhaps we too would benefit from having an advocate for settlement to oppose those counsel who advise us to litigate.

Overcoming the financial disincentive

I would welcome your suggestions for how we might overcome the financial disincentive to settle.

I know of at least one law firm that will quote a fixed fee for handling a case all the way through litigation or until a settlement satisfactory to the client has been produced. If the law firm is of high quality and has a wide base of experience on which to quote the fixed fee, I can see great advantages in this approach. The law firm has an incentive to use its time efficiently and, if possible, to produce a quick settlement satisfactory to the client. (To be sure, because the firm has little incentive to obtain a settlement better than the minimum the client is willing to accept, a client in such a situation has to be on guard.)

Some corporate clients, I realize, do fix with a law firm a monthly or annual ceiling. Although this practice avoids the worst aspects of runaway costs, it does not change the incentives.

More regular means of keeping expenditures under control might also be useful. We should be able to devise a better method than putting a case out for competitive bids. Perhaps we should explore the possibility of having your firm make fairly detailed estimates of monthly costs, followed by monthly reports of actual expenditures. Some corporate clients are now asking their law firms for detailed figures on overhead to satisfy themselves that the high hourly rates they pay in fact go to reward talent, not to reimburse the firm for lavish expenditures.

What techniques does your firm use to keep your lawyers cost-conscious? Is there some way that you could divide profits that would reward lawyers not for bringing in bigger fees but for more accurately estimating the costs and the eventual outcome of each case?

How about awarding a contingent bonus for any lawyer in the office who is able to settle a case to the client's satisfaction against the recommendation of the litigation department? (Such a bonus could come from funds that otherwise would be divided among partners in the litigation department.) Alternatively, maybe we should pay your firm some kind of contingent fee for developing a settlement proposal and convincing both sides that the settlement is preferable to litigation.

Can you think of some way to reduce the pressure on associates in your firm to maximize the billable hours they devote to a big case? It is easier to compare the number of hours that two associates have worked in a year than to compare the quality of their work on different cases for different partners. There must be a risk—in other firms if not in yours—that you will reward associates for spending more time rather than less in accomplishing a given task. I am sure you can tell your best young lawyers from your worst, but on the margin, how do you avoid rewarding inefficiency?

We may want to get some expert consultant in to advise us on how we might best line up the personal financial incentives with the interests the lawyers' work is intended to serve. Perhaps we should look more seriously at other incentives such as prestige or publicity for settling cases, extra vacation time, a bigger office, more assistants, or whatever. Your thinking about this will, I am sure, be helpful.

A two-track approach

It is probably impossible—as well as undesirable—for lawyers to abandon the role of knight in shining armor. But how about creating a second and parallel role for lawyers: the problem solver, the mediator, the conciliator? In our effort to reap the benefits of the adversary process, I propose that for every major case we have one lawyer pursue litigation and another (who might well be a member of your litigation department) explore and develop, at the earliest possible date, the best settlement option obtainable. This "advocate for settlement" would be expected to press on us the reasons for accepting a settlement (or making an offer) and would provide a counterweight to the litigator's partisan bias by pointing out weaknesses in our litigation position.

Just as lawyers are capable of arguing either side of a given case, obviously many are fully capable of litigating a case and negotiating a settlement of it. But this does not mean that they should try to do both at the same time. The psychological orientation of a general engaged in battle is quite different from that of a diplomat engaged in peace negotiations. While a soldier should have little concern for suffering on the other side, a negotiator should empathetically appreciate an adversary's interests. The soldier-lawyer looks back at the causes of the dispute and seeks to demonstrate and vindicate the wrongs committed; the diplomat-lawyer looks forward to the opportunities for reconciling differences.

You may respond to this suggestion by pointing out that having two teams work on the same case would tend to increase rather than reduce legal fees. For the time being at least, I am prepared to take that gamble. My specialist in settlement might well be one of those doing research on the case and helping others prepare it for litigation. I do not propose erecting a Chinese Wall between litigators and settlers. But I do think we would be well served if your firm had specialists in negotiation and settlement – perhaps people with experience as mediators and business negotiators – who were devoting their energies to trying to settle our disputes quickly, wisely, and amicably.

This two-track approach should benefit both the litigator and the settler. The litigator would be under no pressure to pull his punches for fear that an unduly adversarial approach might damage the chances of settlement. And the harder the litigator pursued that option, the more it would strengthen the hand of the lawyer working toward settlement. It would be a classic Mutt and Jeff – good cop, bad cop – approach, but with no deception of any kind.

Of course, both lawyers would not have to be in the same firm. I have thought that if we retain your firm to handle litigation we might develop within the office of our in-house counsel some experts in settlement.

Another alternative, which some companies have adopted and which I would like to consider, would be to hire an outside expert in settlement to work in parallel with your firm's work on the litigation front. There are negotiation experts who might be hired either to mediate (if the other side were interested) or simply to generate a settlement of interest to both sides. Such an expert might have full authority to negotiate on the understanding that no settlement would be binding until the corporation had approved. Before giving such approval we would, of course, expect to hear from litigation counsel.

An organized settlement program

Whether or not we develop or bring in a settlement specialist, your firm could probably do more on a regular basis to reduce the risk of our litigating cases when it would be in our interest to settle them. As a basis for our discussion of specific actions we might ask you to undertake, let me throw out the following ideas:

Develop a settlement strategy. Once we have someone in charge of settlement, that person should carefully identify our interests, assess our opponent's interests, and make an informed guess of the other side's currently perceived choice. What do they think that we are asking them to do? How do they perceive the consequences of their saying yes and of their saying no to what they believe we are asking them to do? (Presumably, they are currently saying no.) How would a choice have to look for them to say yes? How might we change their choice so that a settlement option we would accept might also look acceptable to them?

Such a strategy might well involve lowering the adversary's expectations of the outcome of litigation. The strategy might also involve putting a new proposal on the table, one that meets the adversary's most important interests and lets them look victorious, or at least allows them to avoid feeling taken. A settlement strategy should include a program and schedule that clearly indicate who is going to do what.

Estimate the value of litigating. The more I think about it, the more inexcusable it is that we have not asked you to generate and keep current your firm's best dollar estimate of the outcome of litigation. Of course, it is impossible to be precise, and any figure you might provide would have a fair degree of uncertainty. But you can let us know how wide the range of uncertainty is and how differently various lawyers working on the case estimate the chances of success. I recognize that not all cases are money cases, but many are. All involve financial considerations.

Let me be specific. For every potential money-judgment case of ours that you are handling, I would like to know the maximum dollar figure you believe we should be willing to pay to settle the case, or the least we should be willing to accept in settlement. I am not asking your lawyers to make the business judgment that we should make. Rather, I am asking you to guess as best you can who will win how much and how probable the different outcomes are, and to let me know how uncertain you are about those outcomes.

I would like to receive this figure in writing quarterly (to reflect any changes in assessment) for every case in litigation. We are paying a small fortune for you to pursue litigation. Is there any reason why we should not ask for your best judgment concerning the likely outcomes of our cases?

I would also like you to include in such reports an estimate of legal fees and disbursements for pursuing the case through the various stages of litigation as well as an estimate of how long those various stages are likely to take. These estimates would not be your routine assurance that your statements are based on standard hourly charges and that it is impossible to predict how many hours will be required. Rather, they would include budget figures by months over the course of the expected litigation. My well-founded belief is that although anticipating costs is difficult, you will get steadily better at it – but only if you make budgets and try to live within them.

In making business decisions under conditions of uncertainty, we often use a decision-tree analysis. We estimate when critical events may happen and the odds of one outcome or another happening at that time. We then continue along each branch, repeating the process as we expect different contingencies to occur. I am sure that you do this informally as you consider whether we have a "good" or "excellent" chance of success and what the magnitude of potential judgments might be. The quality of your estimates might improve if you and your colleagues (at first independently) went through the anticipated future of one of our cases assuming that at no point would it be settled.

Let me suggest how that might be done. The first critical point might be when the court considered motions for summary judgment. You would make your best present guess of the chances of the motion's being granted for the plaintiff (say, 10%), granted for the defendant (say, 30%), or denied for both (in this case, 60%). Each possibility would then be pursued. If the plaintiff obtained summary judgment, would the defendant appeal? If so, how long before a decision would be reached? What do we think would be the chances for affirmation or reversal?

Continue similarly for the other two branches of our tree. If the judge denied both motions for summary judgment, how long would it be before we went to trial? What are some realistic outcomes of such a trial? Perhaps there would be a 10% chance that the plaintiff would "win big" (maybe $2 million); a 20% chance that the plaintiff might win a judgment of about $80,000; and a 70% chance that he would lose. We can then go on to another stage, considering the possibility of appeals and the probable outcome of such appeals.

As you estimate the future course of the litigation, you might concurrently estimate what the legal fees and costs would be to go through the different stages. With a little arithmetic (including discounting to find the present value of any future judgments) you could produce the figures that represent the present value of the case for the plaintiff and for the defendant. There is no magic. The calculation simply says that if these assumptions are right, then from a financial point of view, the plaintiff might be well advised to accept X dollars instead of litigating, and that the defen-

dants might be better off paying Y dollars now rather than taking their chances on litigation.

By going through such a process we're all required to think clearly. By having several lawyers make separate estimates, we'd get both a better idea of the range of uncertainty and, presumably, a better final estimate of the value of the case. Such a calculation might take a couple of hours of each lawyer's time. One lawyer could interview the others working on a case, prepare the different decision trees, and then have the lawyers spend an hour or so together discussing their differences and producing a firm estimate.

Can you think of a better way to help us get a handle on just how much we should be willing to pay or to accept in settlement?

Develop a specific settlement option. Once we have done our homework and have talked with the other side, we should be ready to develop a settlement proposal. Of course, there would be tactical questions of when and how to present the proposal to the other side, but at all times we ourselves should know the realistic terms on which we would be prepared to settle the case. To say "it is too early" is no answer. No matter how early it is, once we have had a chance to prepare, there are always some terms on which we should be willing to settle.

Keep a settlement log. We should keep a running log of the settlement process, including your quarterly advice to us on the value of the case, offers made and received, a summary of discussions with the other side, considerations given to formulating and revising settlement offers, and so forth.

An autopsy of all cases. One big step in the advancement of medicine was the autopsy. Until then, doctors buried their mistakes. I would suggest that if we are to become better at deciding when to litigate and when to settle, and on what terms, we need to learn from experience. We do not know how good we are at estimating the value of a case in litigation, and we are unlikely to get better unless we note when we did well and when we did poorly.

I suggest that following the settlement of any case, and following final judgment of any case not settled, we review the history of our settlement efforts to see what we did well and what we might have handled better. The purpose, of course, would not be to assign blame but to learn for the future.

Well, this letter should give us plenty to talk about. After you and a few of your partners have had a chance to read it and think about it, please give me a ring and let's set a time for a brainstorming session, first to generate ideas and then to evaluate them.

Perhaps there are other things we could do to improve the working relationship between our two institutions. A couple of law firms I know have invited officers of some of their corporate clients to participate in training sessions on negotiation and settlement being held for lawyers in the firm. The joint exploration of expectations and assumptions proved illuminating. Joint simulation exercises helped to generate a common language for ongoing dialogue and gave each a better and very real understanding of the other's concerns.

Some of us here have discussed the idea of inviting one or two lawyers from your firm to spend six months or a year working here at the corporation, and perhaps having a lawyer from our general counsel's office spend six months or so working within your firm. Maybe we should meet for lunch regularly a few times a year, not to discuss any particular case but to consider such ideas as well as other things we might do that would improve our effectiveness in working together.

If for some reason you are not interested in talking about such things, please do let me know — and we can talk about that.

As ever,

Roger Fisher

Reprint 85204

The high cost of justice

I burn a man's corn house, and thereby, according to the verdict of an impartial and sworn jury, damage the man $500; he cannot, by the laws of Georgia, realize the verdict. He must pay a tribute of $150 to a lawyer for pleading for him. Again, you held my note for $1,000 for value received. I confess the claim to be just; yet you cannot collect it by the laws of Georgia without paying a tribute of $50 to a lawyer. Again, I defraud you out of property to the amount of $1,000; it is well known by some, verily believed by others, and sworn to by yourself, to have been obtained by fraud; yet by the laws of Georgia you cannot receive the amount of me without paying $200 to a lawyer. Again, a man wills his property in truth and verity according to justice; but someone of the heirs imagines it ought to have been dealt out differently, and institutes a suit for a change of the dividends; the innocent as well as the guilty must fee a lawyer, and thus the estate is consumed by the lawyers.

These are a few of the thousands of parallel cases that happen every year in Georgia. Now let us examine the matter. In the first three examples given, we suppose the cases to have been decided according to equity, and for the claimants to have received from the defendants the amount of their claims; consequently they have received $1,600. Out of this sum, they pay the lawyers $400; $1,600 − 400 = $1,200 to the claimants, when justice had awarded them the full $1,600. Now in order for the claimants to realize the just claims of $1,600, they must receive $2,000 from the defendants: $2,000 − 400 = $1,600. But justice says defendants owe only $1,600, and cost of suit; and to exact $2,000 from them will be $400 too much; and you had as well exact that amount from any other person or persons; for when defendant shall have satisfied the demands of justice, he becomes an innocent person. He has atoned to the law for violating its sacred ties, in paying the cost of the suit; he has satisfied the demand of the claimant; and who has any right to demand anything more?

Yet the $400 must be paid; and who has it to pay? The claimant out of his rightful demands and rightful property has it to pay; and to whom? To the lawyer.

Why, what has the lawyer done to entitle him to any part of the claimant's property? Why, he read the law, and made that profession his study; and it was taken for granted by the people, that he was better qualified to make laws for the good of community than a man of any other profession; consequently, the people sent him to the legislature to enact laws for them; and what is the result? He leaves the interest of his confiding constituents out of mind; consults his own individual interest; makes the laws as complicated as his ingenuity can devise; comes home and declares he has done the best he could for the land; and yet the laws are so complicated that no conjuror can ferret them, nor any two lawyers agree upon one point.

From
John W. Pitts,
Eleven Numbers Against Lawyer Legislation and Fees at the Bar, Written and Printed Expressly for the Benefit of the People, n.p., January 1843.

Customers and Financiers

IDEAS FOR ACTION

Eight ways to save a disintegrating sale

Negotiating with a Customer You Can't Afford to Lose

by Thomas C. Keiser

"I like your product, but your price is way out of line. We're used to paying half that much!"

"Acme's going to throw in the service contract for nothing. If you can't match that, you're not even in the running."

"Frankly, I think we've worked out a pretty good deal here, but now you've got to meet my boss. If you thought I was tough..."

"Tell you what: If you can drop the price by 20%, I'll give you the business. Once you're in our division, you know, you'll have a lock on the whole company. The volume will be huge!"

"I can't even talk to you about payment schedule. Company policy is ironclad on that point."

"Look here, at *that* price, you're just wasting my time! I thought this was a serious bid! Who do you think you're talking to, some green kid?"

This wasn't supposed to happen. You've invested a lot of time earning a customer's trust and goodwill.

Thomas C. Keiser is senior vice president of the Forum Corporation, a training-and-education consulting firm in Boston.

You've done needs-satisfaction selling, relationship selling, consultative selling, customer-oriented selling; you've been persuasive and good-humored. But as you approach the close, your good friend the customer suddenly turns into Attila the Hun, demanding a better deal, eager to plunder your company's margin and ride away with the profits. You're left with a lousy choice: do the business unprofitably or don't do the business at all.

This kind of dilemma is nothing new, of course. Deals fall through every day. But businesses that depend on long-term customer relationships have a particular need to avoid win-lose situations, since backing out of a bad deal can cost a lot of future deals as well. Some buyers resort to hardball tactics even when the salesperson has done a consummate job of selling. The premise is that it costs nothing to ask for a concession. Sellers can always say no. They will still do the deal. But many sellers—especially inexperienced ones—say yes to even the most outrageous customer demands. Shrewd buyers can lure even seasoned salespeople into deals based on emotion rather than on solid business sense. So how do

you protect your own interests, save the sale, and preserve the relationship when the customer is trying to eat your lunch?

Joining battle is not the solution unless you're the only source of whatever the customer needs. (And in that case you'd better be sure you never lose your monopoly.) Leaving the field is an even worse tactic, however tempting it is to walk away from a really unreasonable customer.

Surprisingly, accommodation and compromise are not the answers either. Often a 10% price discount will make a trivial difference in the commission, so the salesperson quickly concedes it. But besides reducing your company's margin significantly, this kind of easy accommodation encourages the customer to expect something for nothing in future negotiations.

Compromise—splitting the difference, meeting the customer halfway—may save time, but because it fails to meet the needs of either party fully it is not the proverbial win-win solution. A competitor who finds a creative way to satisfy both parties can steal the business.

The best response to aggressive but important customers is a kind of

> ## What do you do when your customer turns into Attila the Hun?

assertive pacifism. Refuse to fight, but refuse to let the customer take advantage of you. Don't cave in, just don't counterattack. Duck, dodge, parry, but hold your ground. Never close a door; keep opening new ones. Try to draw the customer into a creative partnership where the two of you work together for inventive solutions that never occurred to any of your competitors.

There are eight key strategies for moving a customer out of a hardball mentality and into a more productive frame of mind.

1. Prepare by knowing your walk-away and by building the number of variables you can work with during the negotiation. Everyone agrees about the walkaway. Whether you're negotiating an arms deal with the Russians, a labor agreement with the UAW, or a contract you can't afford to lose, you need to have a walk-away: a combination of price, terms, and deliverables that represents the least you will accept. Without one, you have no negotiating road map.

Increasing the number of variables is even more important. The more variables you have to work with, the more options you have to offer; the greater your options, the better your chances of closing the deal. With an important customer, your first priority is to avoid take-it-or-leave-it situations and keep the negotiation going long enough to find a workable deal. Too many salespeople think their only variable is price, but such narrow thinking can be the kiss of death. After all, price is one area where the customer's and the supplier's interests are bound to be at odds. Focusing on price can only increase animosity, reduce margin, or both.

Instead, focus on variables where the customer's interests and your own have more in common. For example, a salesperson for a consumer-goods manufacturer might talk to the retailer about more effective ways to use advertising dollars—the retailer's as well as the manufacturer's—to promote the product. By including marketing programs in the discussion, the salesperson helps to build value into the price, which will come up later in the negotiation.

The salesperson's job is to find the specific package of products and services that most effectively increases value for the customer without sacrificing the seller's profit. For example, an automotive parts supplier built up its research and development capacity, giving customers the choice of doing their own R&D in-house or farming it out to the parts supplier. Having this option enabled the supplier to redirect negotiations away from price and toward creation of value in the product-development process. Its revenues and margins improved significantly.

Even with undifferentiated products, you can increase variables by focusing on services. A commodity chemicals salesperson, for example, routinely considered payment options, quantity discounts, bundling with other purchases, even the relative costs and benefits of using the supplier's tank cars or the customer's. Regardless of industry, the more variables you have, the greater your chances of success.

2. When under attack, listen. Collect as much information as possible from the customer. Once customers have locked into a position, it is difficult to move them with arguments, however brilliant. Under these circumstances, persuasion is more a function of listening.

Here's an example from my own company. During a protracted negotiation for a large training and development contract, the customer kept trying to drive down the per diem price of our professional seminar leaders. He pleaded poverty, cheaper competition, and company policy. The contract was a big one, but we were already operating at near capacity, so we had little incentive to shave the per diem even slightly. However, we were also selling books to each seminar participant, and that business was at least as important to us as the services. The customer was not asking for concessions on books. He was only thinking of the per diem, and he was beginning to dig in his heels.

At this point our salesperson stopped talking, except to ask questions, and began listening. She learned a great deal—and uncovered an issue more important to the customer than price.

The customer was director of T&D for a large corporation and a man with career ambitions. To get the promotion he wanted, he needed visibility with his superiors. He was afraid that our professionals would develop their own relationships with his company's top management, leaving him out of the loop. Our salesperson decided to give him the control he wanted. Normally we would have hired free-lancers to fill the gap between our own available

staff and the customer's needs. But in this case she told him he could hire the free-lancers himself, subject to our training and direction. The people we already employed would be billed at their full per diem. He would save money on the free-lancers he paid directly, without our margin. We would still make our profit on the books and the professional services we did provide. He would maintain control.

Moreover, we were confident that the customer was underestimating the difficulty of hiring, training, and managing free-lancers. We took the risk that somewhere down the road

When customers attack, keep them talking.

the customer would value this service and be willing to pay for it. Our judgment turned out to be accurate. Within a year we had obtained the entire professional services contract without sacrificing margin.

It was a solution no competitor could match because no competitor had listened carefully enough to the customer's underlying agenda. Even more important, the buyer's wary gamesmanship turned to trust, and that trust shaped all our subsequent negotiations.

When under attack, most people's natural response is to defend themselves or to counterattack. For a salesperson in a negotiation, either of these will fuel an upward spiral of heated disagreement. The best response, however counterintuitive, is to keep the customer talking, and for three good reasons. First, new information can increase the room for movement and the number of variables. Second, listening without defending helps to defuse any anger. Third, if you're listening, you're not making concessions.

3. Keep track of the issues requiring discussion. Negotiations can get confusing. Customers often get frustrated by an apparent lack of progress; they occasionally go back on agreements already made; they sometimes raise new issues at the last moment. One good way to avoid these problems is to summarize what's already been accomplished and sketch out what still needs to be discussed. Brief but frequent recaps actually help maintain momentum, and they reassure customers that you're listening to their arguments.

Piecemeal negotiating gives the hungry customer one slice at a time.

The best negotiators can neutralize even the most outspoken opposition by converting objections into issues that need to be addressed. The trick is to keep your cool, pay attention to the customer's words and tone, and wait patiently for a calm moment to summarize your progress.

4. *Assert your company's needs.* Effective salespeople always focus on their customers' interests – not their own. They learn to take on a customer perspective so completely that they project an uncanny understanding of the buyer's needs and wants. Too much empathy can work against salespeople, however, because sales bargaining requires a dual focus – on the customer and on the best interests of one's own company. The best negotiating stance is not a single-minded emphasis on customer satisfaction but a concentration on problem solving that seeks to satisfy both parties. Salespeople who fail to assert the needs of their own company are too likely to make unnecessary concessions.

The style of assertion is also extremely important. It must be nonprovocative. "You use our service center 50% more than our average customer. We've got to be paid for that..." will probably spark a defensive reaction from a combative customer. Instead, the salesperson should build common ground by emphasizing shared interests, avoiding inflammatory language, and encour-

aging discussion of disputed issues. This is a better approach: "It's clear that the service center is a critical piece of the overall package. Right now you're using it 50% more than our average customer, and that's driving up our costs and your price. Let's find a different way of working together to keep service costs down and still keep service quality high. To begin with, let's figure out what's behind these high service demands."

5. *Commit to a solution only after it's certain to work for both parties.* If a competitive customer senses that the salesperson is digging into a position, the chances of successfully closing the deal are dramatically reduced. A better approach is to suggest hypothetical solutions. Compare these two approaches in selling a commercial loan:

"I'll tell you what. If you give us all of the currency exchange business for your European branches, we'll cap this loan at prime plus one."

"You mentioned the currency exchange activity that comes out of your European branches. Suppose you placed that entirely with us. We may be able to give you a break in the pricing of the new loan."

The first is likely to draw a counterproposal from a competitive customer. It keeps the two of you on opposite sides of the negotiating table. The second invites the customer to help shape the proposal. Customers who participate in the search for solutions are much more likely to wind up with a deal they like.

Some salespeople make the mistake of agreeing definitively to an issue without making sure the overall deal still makes sense. This plays into the hands of an aggressive customer trying to get the whole loaf one slice at a time. It's difficult to take back a concession. Instead, wrap up issues tentatively. "We agree to do X, provided we can come up with a suitable agreement on Y and Z."

6. *Save the hardest issues for last.* When you have a lot of points to negotiate, don't start with the toughest, even though it may seem logical to begin with the deal killers. After all, why spend time on side is-

sues without knowing whether the thorniest questions can be resolved?

There are two reasons. First, resolving relatively easy issues creates momentum. Suppose you're working with a customer who's bound and determined to skin you alive when it comes to the main event. By starting with lesser contests and finding inventive solutions, you may get the customer to see the value of exploring new approaches. Second, discussing easier issues may uncover additional variables. These will be helpful when you finally get down to the heart of the negotiation.

7. *Start high and concede slowly.* Competitive customers want to see a return on their negotiation investment. When you know that a customer wants to barter, start off with something you can afford to lose. Obviously, game playing has its price. Not only do you train your customers to ask for concessions, you also teach them never to relax their guard on money matters. Still, when the customer really wants to wheel and deal, you have little choice.

The customer too can pay a price for playing games. A classic case involves a customer who always bragged about his poker winnings, presumably to intimidate salespeople before negotiations got started. "I always leave the table a winner," he seemed to be saying. "Say your prayers." What salespeople actually did was raise their prices 10% to 15% before sitting down to negotiate.

Some salespeople make their worst mistake before they ever sit down at the table.

They'd let him win a few dollars, praise his skill, then walk away with the order at a reasonable margin.

A number of studies have shown that high expectations produce the best negotiating results and low expectations the poorest. This is why salespeople must not let themselves be intimidated by the customer who

Two Common Mistakes

Combative buyers are hard enough to handle without provoking them further, yet many salespeople unintentionally annoy buyers to the point of complete exasperation. What's worse, the two most common mistakes crop up most frequently at times of disagreement, the very moment when poking sticks at the customer ought to be the last item on your list of priorities.

The first mistake is belaboring. Some salespeople will repeat a single point until customers begin to feel badgered or heckled. Chances are they heard you the first time. You can also belabor a customer with logic or with constant explanations that seem to suggest that the customer is none too bright.

The second mistake is rebutting every point your customer makes, which is almost certain to lead to an argument—point and counterpoint. Don't say "night" every time your customer says "day," even if you're convinced the customer is wrong.

always bargains every point. Once they lower their expectations, they have made the first concession in their own minds before the negotiation gets under way. The customer then gets to take these premature concessions along with the normal allotment to follow.

A man I used to know—the CEO of a company selling software to pharmacies—always insisted on absolute candor in all customer dealings. He'd begin negotiations by showing customers his price list and saying, "Here's our standard price list. But since you're a big chain, we'll give you a discount." He broke the ice with a concession no one had asked for and got his clock cleaned nearly every time.

The key is always to get something in return for concessions and to know their economic value. Remember that any concession is

likely to have a different value for buyer and seller, so begin by giving things that the customer values highly but that have little incremental cost for your company:

Control of the process
Assurance of quality
Convenience
Preferred treatment in times of product scarcity
Information on new technology (for example, sharing R&D)
Credit
Timing of delivery
Customization
Service

There's an old saying, "He who concedes first, loses." This may be true in a hardball negotiation where the customer has no other potential source of supply. But in most competitive sales situations, the salesperson has to make the first concession in order to keep the deal alive. Concede in small increments, get something in return, and know the concession's value to both sides. Taking time may seem crazy to salespeople who have learned that time is money. But in a negotiation, *not* taking time is money.

8. *Don't be trapped by emotional blackmail.* Buyers sometimes use emotion—usually anger—to rattle salespeople into making concessions they wouldn't otherwise make. Some use anger as a premeditated tactic; others are really angry. It doesn't matter whether the emotion is genuine or counterfeit. What does matter is how salespeople react. How do you deal with a customer's rage and manage your own emotions at the same time?

Here are three different techniques that salespeople find useful in handling a customer who uses anger—wittingly or unwittingly—as a manipulative tactic.

□ Withdraw. Ask for a recess, consult with the boss, or reschedule the meeting. A change in time and place can change the entire landscape of a negotiation.

Author's note: I wish to acknowledge the ideas of Ann Carol Brown, David Berlew, John Carlisle, Greg Crawford, Richard Pascale, Mike Pedler, Neil Rackham, and my colleagues at the Forum Corporation.

□ Listen silently while the customer rants and raves. Don't nod your head or say "uh-huh." Maintain eye contact and a neutral expression, but do not reinforce the customer's behavior. When the tirade is over, suggest a constructive agenda.

□ React openly to the customer's anger, say that you find it unproductive, and suggest focusing on a specific, nonemotional issue. There are two keys to this technique. The first is timing: don't rush the process or you risk backing the customer into a corner from which there is no graceful escape. The second is to insist that the use of manipulative tactics is unacceptable and then to suggest a constructive agenda. Don't be timid. The only way to pull this off is to be strong and assertive.

For example, imagine this response to a customer throwing a fit: "This attack is not constructive. [Strong eye contact, assertive tone.] We've spent three hours working the issues and trying to arrive at a fair and reasonable solution. Now I suggest that we go back to the question of payment terms and see if we can finalize those."

Of course, there is substantial risk in using any of these techniques. If you withdraw, you may not get a second chance. If you listen silently or react ineffectively, you may alienate the customer further. These are techniques to resort to only when the discussion is in danger of going off the deep end, but at such moments they have saved many a negotiation that looked hopeless.

The essence of negotiating effectively with aggressive customers is to sidestep their attacks and convince them that a common effort at problem solving will be more profitable and productive. Your toughest customers will stop throwing punches if they never connect. Your most difficult buyer will brighten if you can make the process interesting and rewarding. The old toe-to-toe scuffle had its points, no doubt. Trading blow for blow was a fine test of stamina and guts. But it was no test at all of imagination. In dealing with tough customers, creativity is a better way of doing business.

Reprint 88605

Growing Concerns

Edited by
Edwin Harwood

You *can* negotiate with venture capitalists

*Harold M. Hoffman
and James Blakey*

If you're an entrepreneur looking for venture capital, you're probably well aware of the frustrations in finding loose purse strings in the financial markets. Your business is too new or your product is still too untried to qualify for conventional intermediate- or long-term debt financing. Or, although you know you might qualify for a loan, you don't want to take on the risk of more debt.

You've already used your savings and borrowed from relatives to get the seed capital you need. And you may have reached the point where you're generating healthy sales figures. But you've still got a long way to go before you can think of a public offering, and you can't finance the growth you want from retained earnings alone.

You need equity capital. If your management has a good track record and your business has the potential to generate a very high return on investment—say 30% to 40% per year—professional venture capitalists may be prepared to fork over high-risk capital of $1 million or more to finance your growth. You don't have to have a high-tech company to qualify; venture capitalists will also invest in conventional businesses that offer high ROI potential. We have recently negotiated venture capital deals involving an oil-drilling equipment manufacturer, a movie distributor, and a financial newsletter publisher, among others.

Because you've heard that money talks when a deal gets struc-

tured, you may worry that if you rock the boat by demanding too much, the venture capital firm will lose interest. That's an understandable attitude; venture capital is hard to get and if you've gotten as far as the negotiating process, you're already among the lucky few.

But that doesn't mean you have to roll over and play dead. A venture capital investment is a business deal that you may have to live with for a long time. Although you'll have to give ground on many issues when you come to the bargaining table, there is always a point beyond which the deal no longer makes sense for you. You must draw a line and fight for the points that really count. The extent to which you can stand your ground will depend, of course, on the leverage you have in the negotiations. If your business already shows a profit or if you're selling a highly desirable service or product, you'll have more bargaining power than if your company is burning up cash because sales are still several years down the road.

Structuring the investment

Before you and the venture capitalists agree to a financing package, you have to settle two important issues: the worth of your business before the VCs put their money in and the

type of securities the VCs will receive in exchange for their investment.

Valuation. Although your company's tangible net worth (book value) may be low or negative, the fair market value may be higher because of proprietary technology, sales potential, or other factors. You can more easily defend the value you place on your company if your projections are prepared with the assistance of a reputable accounting firm. It also helps to bring to the negotiations valuation data for comparable business ventures.

It's important to negotiate hard for a reasonable valuation of your company because the amount of equity you give the VCs will depend largely on that calculation. Let's assume, for instance, that you and the venture capitalists agree that your business is now worth $4 million. Based on this valuation and the company's cash needs, you strike a deal whereby the VCs will invest $1 million. The company's worth accordingly rises to $5 million. The VCs' $1 million should therefore buy the equivalent of 20% of the total post-investment equity outstanding.

Capital structure. When it comes to capital structure, VCs like to have their cake and eat it too: they want equity because that will give them a big slice of the profits if your company succeeds, but they also want debt because debt holders get paid before equity holders if the company fails. So VCs usually invest in redeemable preferred stock or debentures. If things go well, the VCs can convert preferred stock or debentures to common stock. If things go badly, however, they will get paid before you and other holders of common stock.

If you have a choice, try to get the VCs to accept a capital structure that consists entirely of common stock, because it's simpler and keeps the balance sheet clean. Chances are, however, that you won't get them to

Messrs. Hoffman and Blakey are partners of Kronish, Lieb, Weiner and Hellman, a New York City law firm. They specialize in negotiating initial public offerings for private corporations as well as private placements and venture capital for both public and private corporations seeking new financing.

agree to this unless your bargaining position is extremely strong.

In some deals, the VCs ask for a debenture together with warrants that allow them to purchase common stock at a nominal price. Under this arrangement, the VCs really do get to eat their cake and have it too because they don't have to convert their debt to equity. They'll regain 100% of their investment when the debt is repaid and still share in the equity appreciation of the company when they exercise their warrants.

Although the documents used to create debentures, preferred stock, and warrants are usually so much boilerplate, they must still be reviewed with care. One consideration is the legal structure of the investment, because the laws that govern what a corporation can do with its securities vary from state to state. Some states, New York for example, do not permit issuance of preferred stock that is redeemable at the holder's option. Antidilution and liquidation provisions, which are discussed in the next section, can have unexpected effects if not carefully crafted. Subordination provisions in debentures are also important, because your trade creditors and institutional lenders will expect clear-cut language placing the VCs' claim to the company's assets behind their own.

Protecting the investment

Many venture capitalists seek to protect their investments by asking for antidilution, performance/forfeiture, and other protective provisions. Their concern over preserving the value of their capital is legitimate. At the same time, you should review these provisions carefully to make sure they are fair to you and any other founders.

Antidilution provisions. The VCs' preferred stock and debentures will be convertible, at their option, into common stock at a specified rate. Obviously, neither you nor the VCs expect the value of your company's stock to drop, but you can't control the value the market places on your business. If your company begins to do poorly and you need more money, you may have

no choice but to sell off new equity more cheaply than in the past. Once they have bought in, the VCs will want to be sure that later stock issuances won't water down the value of their investment.

Don't forget to negotiate for yourself.

Antidilution protection does not mean that an investment must always be convertible into a fixed percentage ownership share of the company, without regard to intervening growth and investment. As long as any new common stock is sold at a price equal to or higher than the rate at which the VCs can convert into common stock, their investment won't be diluted economically. Although their slice of the pie will shrink, the pie itself will grow at least commensurately. But if new common stock is sold for less than that price, the pie won't expand as quickly as the VCs' slice shrinks—and the VCs' investment will consequently be diluted. To guard against this outcome, the VCs' conversion right will usually include an antidilution adjustment, or "ratchet."

There are two kinds of ratchets, full and weighted. With a full ratchet, the rate for converting the VCs' debentures or preferred stock into common is reduced to the lowest price at which any common is subsequently sold—a situation that can have drastic consequences for you and other founders. If the company sells a single share cheaply, *all* the VCs' securities suddenly become convertible into common at that lower rate. The VCs can very quickly end up with the lion's share of the company.

Let's return to the situation in which a VC firm has invested $1 million and received a 20% share of your now $5 million company. On this basis, if your company started out with four million shares outstanding, the VCs' $1 million will be initially convertible at the rate of $1 per share into one million shares of stock (or 20% of the five million shares outstanding after conversion).

Under a full ratchet, if your company sells one share of common stock for 25 cents, the conversion rate of the VCs' securities will drop to that price. The VCs' $1 million will now buy four million common shares. After conversion, the VCs will thus own four million out of eight million shares, or 50% rather than 20% of the company. So even though the sale of this single share would have no material dilutive effect on the VCs' investment, under a full ratchet provision such a sale would severely reduce the value of the equity that you and any other founders hold.

The more common and equitable approach is to negotiate a weighted ratchet whereby the conversion rate for the VCs' shares is adjusted down to the weighted average price per share of all outstanding common after the issuance of cheaper stock. If only a few cheap shares are issued, the downward adjustment will be minor. The usual method is to treat all shares outstanding before the cheaper dilutive issuance as if they were floated at the initial conversion price.

Mechanics aside, negotiating the antidilution adjustment carefully is important because its purpose is to place any dilutive effect of a future stock issuance on you and the other founders, not on the VCs. You can, however, seek to moderate the effect of such a provision. For example, you can ask that any common shares issuable to the VCs on conversion of their preferred stock or debentures be included in the number of outstanding shares used for calculating the adjustment. This will spread the impact of a dilutive issuance over a larger number of shares. You can also request that any common shares sold cheaply to officers, directors, employees, or consultants—a customary practice in start-up situations, and one that benefits all investors—will not trigger the antidilution adjustment.

The risk posed by an antidilution provision, especially one with a full ratchet, is that you and other founders can be squeezed out if the company runs into serious financial problems. If the company's market value falls far enough below the dollar value of the VCs' original investment, an antidilution adjustment will not only wipe out your equity but can actually prevent you from seeking new investors, unless you can get the VCs to waive their antidilution rights.

Performance/forfeiture provisions. As a condition for investment, the VCs may subject your stock – including stock you acquired years earlier – to a performance/forfeiture arrangement. Under this provision, if the company fails to meet certain earnings or other targets, you must forfeit some or all of your stock.

A performance/forfeiture provision serves several purposes. For one, it protects the VCs from paying for an overvalued company. The valuation of unseasoned companies usually relies heavily on speculative sales and earnings projections. If you overestimated operating results by a wide margin, the VCs will have paid too much for their share of the company.

Because sales and earnings forecasts are only projections, not promises, the VCs cannot sue the company if management fails to perform as expected. But if you've agreed to a performance/forfeiture provision, they can compensate themselves by increasing their ownership interest at your expense.

Another reason the VCs may want this provision is that if the company doesn't do well, it will be free to reissue the forfeited stock to any new executives brought in without diluting the VCs' holdings. The performance/forfeiture provision also serves as a golden handcuff: it motivates you and any other founders to work hard and stick with the business.

If your company is in an early stage of development, you may have to place a large portion of your stock at risk of forfeiture because the company's future is still very uncertain. As time passes, your enterprise is more likely to gain in value and enjoy a more predictable future. Then you can legitimately refuse to agree to a forfeiture provision on the grounds that the company's valuation is realistic, based on past performance.

What should you negotiate for? If the VCs insist on including a for-feiture provision, you may be able to persuade them to include stock bonuses for performance that beats your sales and earnings projections. If you're expected to forfeit stock for failing to hit 80% of the sales or earnings targets in your business plan, for example, it stands to reason that you should get an equivalent bonus if you exceed those targets.

Employment contracts. The terms of the founders' employment are always part of the financing arrangement. The VCs will want an agreement covering your salary, bonuses, benefits, and the circumstances under which you can quit or be fired by the board.

It may come as a shock to realize that the VCs are making an investment in the company, not you. As companies grow, they often require professional management skills that you and the other founding entrepreneurs may lack. The time may come when the VCs think you're no longer competent to run the business and decide to terminate your employment.

If the VCs are buying a controlling interest, you should seek an employment contract of reasonable duration – at least two to three years. If your business is well past the start-up stage, you may want to negotiate a longer term of at least five years.

There is, however, one potential drawback: a long-term contract may prevent you from leaving the company to do other things. If the company is doing poorly, the VCs may want you to stay and keep trying after you've decided to move on. Although the VCs can't prevent your departure, they may be able to sue you for breach of contract. Also, your contract may preclude your working in the same industry once you quit.

The grounds on which the board can terminate your employment should be fully spelled out and kept narrow in scope. Good examples of reasonable and narrow grounds include a felony conviction, theft of company property, or chronic failure to carry out reasonable instructions from the board despite repeated requests. If you're fired and you decide to sue for wrongful termination, you'll find it easier to prove your case if specific grounds were written into your contract.

Here are some other provisions to check for in the employment agreement before signing the deal:

☐ Are you assured adequate advance notice of the board's decision not to renew your original contract or its decision to renew but on terms that are less beneficial to you?

☐ Are you getting an adequate severance package, including extended insurance coverage?

☐ If you're obligated not to compete with the company after termination, what is the scope and duration of your obligation? Are you only prohibited from hiring away employees and soliciting business from the company's established customers, or must you leave your line of business altogether?

☐ Is the company required to buy back any or all of your stock if you are terminated, or does it have the option of doing so? How will the price be determined? You should try to negotiate for an option to sell your stock back to the company according to a fixed formula (for instance, a certain multiple of earnings) in the event that you're fired. Many companies resist having to buy back equity, so you may have trouble cashing out unless you include this option in your contract.

You may, of course, persuade the VCs to accept an employment agreement that does not permit the board to terminate you. Moreover, your postemployment rights and obligations may vary depending on whether you quit of your own accord, did something egregiously wrong, or were simply fired because the board was unhappy with your performance.

Control. You will have to let the VCs share in running your company. In all likelihood you'll be required to retain a nationally recognized accounting firm to certify your annual financial statements. You may also have to accept the addition of managers recommended by the VCs to cover areas of the business they think need improvement. The VCs will usually place one of their representatives on your board and possibly more, depending on their ownership interest. Important decisions like whether to merge, liquidate assets, or sell stock will require their consent even if they have only a minority position.

> *If your business shows a profit, you'll have more bargaining power.*

Nevertheless, there is some room for negotiation when it comes to control provisions. If you and other founders agree to a deal that leaves you with a minority interest, ask for no less than the VCs would probably demand: that they guarantee you board representation and obtain your consent before making any major business decisions.

Shareholder agreements. In almost all deals, the VCs will also want the company's founders to enter into a shareholders' agreement. Such an agreement may require the founders to vote for one or more directors of the VCs' choosing. It may also grant the VCs majority control of the board if the business runs into serious trouble, even if they have only a minority interest.

Shareholder agreements can also govern the sale of stock, including newly issued shares. Under most arrangements, the seller is required to offer the stock to the company or other parties to the agreement (insiders) before selling to outsiders. The VCs may also want to include a cosale stipulation that would oblige any selling shareholder to arrange for the other insiders to participate in the sale to an extent proportionate to their holdings.

Usually the company is also bound to the shareholder agreement. Depending on the agreement, the company may have to offer stock to the VCs, to all parties to the agreement, or

to all current shareholders (in proportion to their holdings) before issuing any new stock to a third party. Because this preemptive right to purchase additional shares allows investors to maintain an absolute percentage interest in the company, the VCs are almost certain to insist on having it. You should ask for no less for yourself. If the company issues more shares, you should have the same opportunity as the VCs to retain your current percentage of ownership.

Disclosure. Before the VCs hand over the money, they will doubtless want extensive disclosure about your company. You'll be asked to verify that the company is in good standing, has paid its taxes, and is in compliance with all laws. You must also establish that the company's financial statements are correct and that it has no agreements or contingent obligations other than those referred to in an attached disclosure schedule. You should seek, whenever possible, to narrow the scope of these representations and qualify them as being to the best of your knowledge at the time. Inclusion of any matter you think may apply will avoid later argument by the VCs that you failed to disclose relevant information.

It's a good idea to negotiate for a cushion in your favor, so that if there are omissions in your representations that later cost the company no more than, say, $50,000, the omissions won't be considered a breach of the representation. In addition, ask for a time limit on your representations about the company—they should not apply for more than six months to a year after the deal has been closed.

Cashing out the investment

In any venture capital deal, the VCs will be looking ahead to the day when they can liquidate their investment in your company. They'll likely want provisions written into the agreement that will give them the opportunity to cash out on favorable terms at a time of their choosing.

Registration rights. Federal securities laws (and the "blue sky"

laws of many states) prohibit you from selling an interest in your company unless you have either filed a registration statement with the SEC or qualified for an exemption from registration. Registration is an expensive process, which most companies avoid by getting a "private placement" exemption. To qualify for this exemption, your company must approach no more than a small number of wealthy and sophisticated investors.

The securities laws also impose legal restrictions that generally will prevent the VCs and other shareholders from reselling any stock acquired under a private placement exemption for at least two years, and may limit the amount that can be sold without a registration even after that period. Accordingly, the VCs will probably want the right to require the company to register their stock at the company's expense.

The VCs' registration rights may include either piggyback rights, which require the company to include the VCs' shares only if the company itself decides to file a registration statement, or demand rights, which allow the VCs to force the company to file a registration statement covering their shares. In granting piggyback rights to the VCs, check to make sure that the provision includes you and the other shareholders on an equal basis and that the company's ability to grant future piggyback rights is not limited.

Demand rights should be negotiated with even greater care. Because of the expense, try to limit the VCs to one request for a demand registration, or they may keep the company in constant registration. Also, try to get them to agree to postpone exercising this right until after the company's first public offering. Without this restriction, the VCs may be able to force the company to go public before it can afford the heavy reporting and other burdens imposed on publicly held companies.

If you agree to registration rights, you should be sure to include yourself. As an insider, you will probably be subject to transfer limitations under the securities laws regardless of how long you have held your stock. If you don't have a contractual right to be included in a registration, you may find yourself squeezed out of a public offering by investors who do. Furthermore, be sure that the company is obliged to pay your registration expenses. If it isn't, you will have to pay a proportionate share of what can be an enormous bill—for lawyers, accountants, printers, state securities filings, and underwriters' expenses. (Certain states will not permit the company to pay insiders' registration expenses; if your underwriter wants to offer stock in those states, you may have to waive your registration rights.)

Liquidation and merger provisions. Provisions governing the liquidation or merger of your business are important, yet they are often overlooked. If you are not careful, you may unwittingly agree to a provision that harms you or creates windfall gains for the VCs in the event of a merger or other corporate combination.

If, for example, preferred shareholders are allowed to treat a merger like a liquidation, they can demand a cash payment at the time of the merger. This kind of provision makes the merger less appealing to a potential partner. It can kill a deal outright, or at least give the preferred shareholders leverage to extract other concessions— usually at your expense.

Clauses relating to liquidation preferences should also get careful scrutiny. Liquidation preferences specify the order in which holders of different classes of securities get paid and how much of the liquidation proceeds they can collect before other investors are repaid. Under some preference provisions, the VCs not only receive 100% of their initial investment back but also have the right to share in any remaining proceeds, as if the investment consisted of common stock.

One risk to you of such a provision is that the VCs may be better off if the company liquidates than if it remains in operation. While the company remains in business, the VCs can only participate as either holders of preferred stock or debt or holders of common stock. On liquidation, they can participate as both. Moreover, liquidation provisions don't apply just in cases of failure, when there is nothing left to distribute; companies are sometimes liquidated even when business is good. And the VCs may control the decision whether to liquidate.

Modifying rights. To avoid a situation in which a right given the VCs can block a transaction crucial to the company's survival, it's important to include a provision that allows the VCs' rights to be changed. The VCs' rights cannot be modified without their consent. Because you may have investments from a number of VCs, and you may therefore not be able to get a unanimous decision, you should try to get the VCs to agree in advance that a majority or two-thirds count of their combined interest can waive the VCs' rights on behalf of all.

The key to weathering the venture capital process is to put the transaction in perspective. When it's all over, your young and not particularly bankable company will have a large sum of cash to put to work. Although some things the VCs demand may seem ridiculous, burdensome, or even insulting, you can't expect to get that amount of money without a lot of strings attached—and some of the things they make you do may even be good for you.

Remember that even though funding risky ventures is their business, venture capitalists will do all they can to avoid losing their capital. Expect them to be tough negotiators.

But this doesn't mean that you don't have the right to protect your interests in the deal. You won't get your way on every provision, but you should be able to persuade the VCs to see matters from your point of view on some. The best strategy is to try to fight any provisions that will keep you from running your company effectively or that are clearly unfair to you, and not wrestle too hard over the others.

Your negotiations should be guided by a spirit of fairness and respect for each other's legitimate interests. Properly handled, these negotiations can build a foundation of trust and cooperation from the very start— giving your business the best possible chance for success. ▽

Reprint 87207

How to negotiate a term loan

A successful strategy depends on defensive preparation

Jasper H. Arnold III

Despite the proliferation of services available to finance ongoing operations, the fundamental source of capital for all companies remains banks. And negotiations with banks always boil down to a contract between those who have the money and those who need it. Most growing companies need to seek external financing at some point, and a very common form of this financing is the bank term loan. These loans often carry with them restrictive covenants that can unduly hamper management and increase the risk of a default.

Unfortunately, for many managers these negotiations are pitted with more uncertainties and difficulties than other types of contracts. The responsibility weighs heavily on a small company manager who may lack financial expertise, especially if the company's future is uncertain. An officer in a more financially sophisticated corporation may understand the process – but not know how to best protect the diverse interests of one part of the company from the demands of the others.

Talks with participants on both sides of the loan process, coupled with his own banking experience, give the author a knowledgeable perspective on how to turn the process around to the company's advantage. His advice for the manager is to plan a negotiating strategy. By learning to think like a banker, you will be better able to obtain a loan agreement that meets your needs without putting a stranglehold on your business.

Mr. Arnold is senior vice president and manager of the credit department at First City National Bank of Houston. A specialist in corporate finance and commercial banking, he has had extensive term lending experience. He has published several articles on banking and corporate finance and has taught in the department of finance at the University of Houston.

Financial managers responsible for negotiating term loans from commercial banks often feel confronted by a stone wall – the banker's restrictions (*restrictive covenants*) on the company to ensure repayment. While the ultimate objectives are easily understood (getting the least expensive funds under the fewest restrictions), achieving them is not. Since the first caveman loaned a spear to a friend only to have it returned the next day broken into little pieces, lenders have been cautious in dealing with borrowers. Moreover, lenders know they have a certain power over borrowers and have turned it into a mystique. Unlike the case in other contract negotiations, many borrowers feel they have few, if any, cards to play – that is, they have to take most of what the banker decides to dish out.

After years of participating in the loan negotiation process, I have found it not as one-sided as it appears. The banker does *not* always win; savvy companies realize that, as in every other aspect of the business, success depends on negotiating strategy.

To help companies devise an effective negotiating strategy, I studied 50 requests for term loans made at eight New York and regional banks. The study, a review of the borrower's financial statements and the final loan agreements, confirms that managers winding up with the best (least restrictive) loan package:

Author's note: Bankers' restrictions are imposed via a formal, written loan agreement, which typically contains two distinct types of covenants, affirmative and negative. I review both, as well as the structure of a typical agreement, in the *Appendix*. Throughout the article, I deal solely with negative covenants, since they are the most restrictive and vigorously debated.

Learn to think like the banker and identify the bank's objectives.

Meet the banker's objectives in making the loan with the least damage to their own position.

Set a list of priorities on the restrictions wanted by the banker, so that they can give in on one or two of them without hindering the company's strategy.

Influence the banker to relax or withdraw noncrucial restrictions.

Inside the banker's head

First, let's look at the two sides in this contest. At the outset the bank's perspective is built on an objective and subjective analysis of the borrowing company's financial position. The analysis rests on that well-established tenet – permanent asset needs should be financed with permanent capital. When permanent capital takes the form of long-term debt, the lender wants to find out how healthy the borrower's long-term earning power is. So the bank asks for financial information as a start – historical financial statements (typically five years) as well as a forecast of your company's income statement, balance sheet, and the sources and uses of funds statements for each year.

The bank's principal and interest will be returned from the future stream of earnings before interest and taxes (EBIT). (Normally, a bank calculates EBIT as *sales* less *cost of sales* less *selling, general, and administrative expenses.*) Consequently, the bank wants to learn the extent of business risk – in other words, how much the future EBIT stream could vary. Another important element is understanding the borrower's industry – both the company's strengths and weaknesses and its overall strategy. (While EBIT is available to cover interest expense, principal payments, not being tax deductible, must be paid out of the net income stream. Moreover, annual principal payments cannot be made out of "cash flow" [net income + depreciation] unless the borrower can forego replacing depreciated fixed assets.)

Banks consider some lines of business inherently risky and this will influence the analysis, but the financial forecast becomes the primary basis on which the banker quizzes the manager to determine the degree of business risk. The banker also uses the forecast to establish how restrictive the loan will be.

Bankers also put considerable emphasis on the company's historical earnings record as an indicator of business risk. Wide fluctuations in profits or net losses – or consistently thin profit margins – usually lead to an assessment of high business risk.

After the EBIT stream, the company's balance sheet is the most important financial indicator because the assets are the bank's secondary source of repayment if earnings are not adequate to repay the loan. Therefore, the assessment of balance sheet strength or weakness hinges on the extent to which the banker thinks the loan is recoverable if assets must be sold.

Judgment is largely based on a few key ratios. For example, the current ratio or net working capital position represents the amount of liquid assets the company has available to repay debts. The banker also investigates fixed asset liquidity, important in the event of financial distress or bankruptcy.

Another key balance sheet variable is the company's margin of safety (i.e., the extent to which it is leveraged). To a banker, a company with a total liabilities-to-equity ratio of 1 to 1 can suffer a 50% deterioration in asset value and still repay a loan. If leverage is at a 3-to-1 ratio, however, creditors can only tolerate a 25% shrinkage in asset value. Moreover, since the size of annual principal and interest payments increases as leverage rises, the greater the leverage the greater the chance EBIT will not cover these payments.

The making of restrictions

Bankers use these simple financial indicators to determine the scope and severity of the restrictions placed on a potential borrower. The five possible types of restrictions include cash flow control, strategy control, the default "trigger," balance sheet maintenance, and asset preservation.

Cash flow control

The first source of restrictions comes directly from an analysis of cash flow. A company may want to build its assets so rapidly or pay such excessive dividends that the banker questions whether the EBIT stream will be sufficient to service the loan. In this case, repayment must come from a refinancing by another creditor or an equity sale. If the bank is confident that the company's earnings record and balance sheet will be strong enough to permit refinancing, it will not seek to control the company's cash flow. However, even when refinancing appears possible, bankers will usually limit excessive dividends and stock repurchases to preserve the company's equity base.

Strategy control

The lender may try to control future strategy if he or she believes that the company's resources are ill-matched with the opportunities and risks present in the environment—or when a particular strategy requires an imprudent degree of leverage or illiquidity. Resulting covenants either prohibit managers from implementing the strategy or force them to modify it. In such cases, bankers usually want to reduce the total amount of money invested in a particular product market or spread the investment out over a longer time period, either by limiting capital expenditures and acquisitions or by writing in a debt-to-equity test.

The infamous trigger

One of the most feared aspects of restrictions is the bank's right to call the loan, or trigger a default. The readiness of the trigger depends on the strength of the balance sheet and the degree of business risk—that is, the potential variability in EBIT. Losses erode company assets by reducing the net working capital and the equity base. In that event (or possibly if profitability declines), the banker wants the right to call the entire loan for repayment before deterioration advances. If the company cannot repay the loan, the bank has legal recourse on the assets.

Banks, however, seldom pull the dreaded trigger. Such action usually means bankruptcy for the company, adverse publicity for the bank, and a time-consuming, costly legal proceeding for both parties. In most cases, if the restrictions trigger a default the loan is not called; instead, this imminent possibility forces the borrower to return to the bargaining table. The banker then wants a proposal for corrective action. In return for continuing the loan, the bank can boost the interest-rate demand collateral as compensation for the risk or else rewrite the covenants.

Balance sheet maintenance

A company can harm its balance sheet by excessive leveraging or by financing fixed assets

Examples of the versatility of covenants

Debt-equity ratio	Net worth minimum
Limits the ability of management to leverage the company.	Causes a default if losses occur.
Restricts expansion of assets in traditional or new markets if this expansion must be financed with debt.	Restricts dividend payments.
Limits dividend payments.	**Interest coverage ratio**
Triggers a default in the event of losses.	Causes a default if losses occur.
	Limits the ability of management to leverage the company.
Current ratio or minimum net working capital	**Capital expenditure restrictions**
Keeps management from borrowing short term to finance long-term assets.	Conserves cash within the company.
Limits dividend payments, capital expenditures, and investments because such cash outflows are a use of working capital in the flow-of-funds sense.	Keeps the borrower from expanding in particular markets or product lines.
Triggers a default in the event of losses because losses are a use of working capital.	

with short-term loans, both of which reduce its net working-capital position and liquidity. To keep the borrower from wantonly employing short-term credit, lenders impose a current ratio and/or net working-capital minimum. Also included is a debt-to-equity limit or even a prohibition on additional borrowings.

Asset preservation

Because bankers regard assets as the ultimate source of repayment, they do not want to see a significant portion sold or pledged to other creditors. So, unless the loan is secured, lenders will write in a limit on the extent to which companies can pledge assets (a "negative pledge clause").

Even if the company can put up sufficient collateral, the bank will restrict the sale of assets to forestall disposal for less than their value or for securities that could prove worthless. The bank will place limits on asset sales or require that any sale be made at fair market value in cash and that the proceeds be used to reduce the loan or to acquire replacement assets.

How the restrictions are set

Using this general information, you can see how to chart your initial negotiating strategy. In the *Exhibit*, I illustrate the minimum objectives the banker must achieve, depending on the degree of a particular company's business risk and balance sheet strength. Six principal rules of loan negotiation hold:

The banker will always require certain balance sheet standards. At a minimum, management will be unable to leverage assets too highly or use excessive short-term liabilities to finance long-term assets.

There will always be a trigger. Despite the fact that the banker will probably never call the loan, the presence of a trigger gives the bank the power to take over the company's assets as a result of poor earnings performance.

Assets will be preserved. No banker wants to see the assets of a company sold – or pledged to another creditor.

Restrictions on cash flow vary. Bankers feel comfortable when companies with good prospects and healthy balance sheets can call on outside capital to service debt. Yet they are concerned lest management authorize excessive dividends or buy back large amounts of stock, so they include a very loose limit on dividends or rely on a debt-to-equity or a net working-capital test for control. A company with a weak balance sheet or high business risk will encounter demands to ensure that most of the cash it generates is used for repayment instead of dividends or capital expenditures.

Tightness of restrictions depends on the level of business risk and strength of the balance sheet. "Tightness" is the degree to which the balance sheet and income statement tests track existing and forecast levels. The tighter the covenant, the more restrictive the control on management's freedom to pay cash out, leverage the company, or incur losses.

Strategy control applies across the board. With a company having a high degree of business risk and a weak balance sheet, the bank will try to restrain strategic movement that it deems inappropriate. More credit-worthy candidates will suffer fewer restrictions if the banker does not like the corporate strategy but will be faced with more sensitive triggers that can be quickly set off if the strategy fails.

Some examples of different negotiations help illustrate the various possibilities.

An oil field pump manufacturer (Quadrant II) wanted a five-year term loan of several million dollars to double the size of its manufacturing facility and to provide working capital to expand sales. The company had been plagued with low profit margins, inventory control problems, and operating inefficiencies. To retain market share, however, the expansion was necessary even though the added production and sales capacity might exacerbate the problems.

The banker thought the balance sheet was reasonably strong. To maintain that strength, he set a long-term debt-equity limit and a current ratio minimum. Since the borrower's strategy exposed it to much business risk, however, the banker wanted a quick default triggered if losses occurred. So he set a minimum net worth covenant that increased every year and closely tracked the forecast levels. The banker also thought that the company's ultimate profitability was too uncertain for him to risk refinancing as a source of required principal payments, so he imposed capital expenditure, investment, and dividend restrictions. The bank included a negative pledge clause and a prohibition on asset sales of more than $1 million in any fiscal year.

Most of the successful companies in Quadrant I were members of the *Fortune* "1000" industrials. The lenders were willing to let these companies do as they pleased if balance sheet ratios remained within certain bounds and profits did not drop. Therefore, they set debt-to-equity maximums and current ratio or working capital restrictions well outside of the forecast levels. These covenants, taken together with either a net worth minimum or a coverage test, also provided a trigger. Negative pledge clauses were always used and asset sales were limited.

A regional chain of steak houses wanted financing to open up several new restaurants within one year in a distant market where it was unknown. The expansion, which would more than double the chain's size, required high leveraging, and management wanted to expand at a time when some of the new restaurants had not yet realized satisfactory profits. Further, restaurant business assets are viewed as highly illiquid if sold under distress conditions. Thus, the bank saw a rapid growth strategy as too risky – and set restrictions to slow growth.

A moderate debt-to-equity ratio would curtail expansion until the existing restaurants generated enough new equity to support the borrowings necessary to open the new units. This test simultaneously ensured holding the company's leverage to a satisfactory level. Unwilling to rely on a refinancing for repayment and determined to control the company's cash, the banker prohibited dividends and long-term investments. The creditor used a debt-to-equity test as a

Exhibit	Determinants of the objectives and tightness of restrictive covenants	
Covenant objectives	1 Cash flow control 2 Strategy control 3 Trigger	4 Balance sheet maintenance 5 Asset preservation

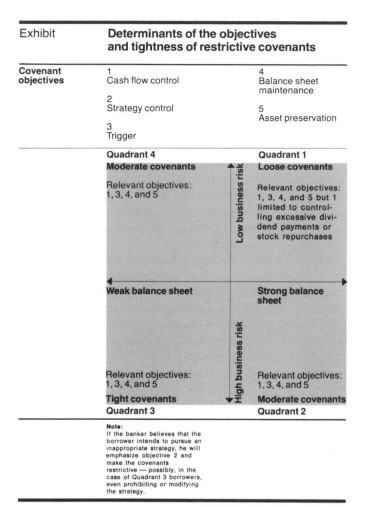

Quadrant 4
Moderate covenants

Relevant objectives:
1, 3, 4, and 5

Quadrant 1
Loose covenants

Relevant objectives:
1, 3, 4, and 5 but 1 limited to controlling excessive dividend payments or stock repurchases

Low business risk

Weak balance sheet

Strong balance sheet

High business risk

Relevant objectives:
1, 3, 4, and 5

Tight covenants
Quadrant 3

Relevant objectives:
1, 3, 4, and 5

Moderate covenants
Quadrant 2

Note:
If the banker believes that the borrower intends to pursue an inappropriate strategy, he will emphasize objective 2 and make the covenants restrictive — possibly, in the case of Quadrant 3 borrowers, even prohibiting or modifying the strategy.

trigger if losses occurred and added a cash-flow-coverage ratio. The loan agreement did not restrict the company's extension of collateral to other creditors, but it did restrict excessive asset sales.

Forge your own strategy

You can use the model in the *Exhibit* to determine what will influence the banker in your particular case and what restrictions the banker is likely to impose. Keep in mind the following guidelines:

1 Consider your earnings history over the past five years. Losses, consistently low profit margins, or very volatile earnings usually indicate a great degree of business risk.

2 Ask yourself whether the variables that determine EBIT (e.g., raw material costs, sales volume, product price, foreign exchange rates) will change over the life of the loan and cause severe declines in earnings.

3 After taking into account the loan, look at the existing and forecast balance sheet ratios such as the debt-to-equity ratio and the current ratio. Do they indicate an illiquid or highly leveraged condition? (If a company's forecast is based on assumptions that are overgenerous in view of historical results, a banker will frequently draw up a forecast with more conservative assumptions. Try it yourself. In that case, can the debt be serviced? What happens to the leverage and liquidity ratios?)

4 Considering the types of assets the company owns, the net working capital level, and the margin of safety for creditors (leverage), could the bank get repayment if the company's assets were liquidated? If the answer is yes, then yours is a strong-balance-sheet company. If the answer is no or maybe, then yours is a weak-balance-sheet company.

Supplement this analysis by questioning the banker before negotiations start. First ask about the bank's preliminary judgments on the balance sheet, historical earnings performance, and the business risk of the company. Then inquire about the soundness of your proposed strategies.

Be careful. Probe responses and always read between the lines. Following initial conversations, make sure the banker receives any additional information necessary about the company – its products, markets, and strategy.

Once you have a good idea as to the banker's objectives, evaluate each possible restriction. To do this properly, you must understand how the more popular restrictive covenants are used and how they can simultaneously accomplish one or more objectives. The ruled insert gives a good example of their versatility.

For example, the current ratio and minimum net-working-capital tests give the bank a broad range of control. They simultaneously provide a trigger, control cash flow, and maintain the balance sheet. These covenants, particularly the current ratio minimum, are the most often violated – simply because almost every financial event or managerial action affects the company's working capital.

Identify costly restrictions

During negotiations the manager must try to minimize the impact of restrictions that might unduly hamper management or easily trigger a violation before the company's financial situation has seriously deteriorated. The most useful tool to determine whether restrictions are too tight is your financial forecast. For example, suppose the bank wants to impose a long-term debt-equity limit of .75 to 1, and you forecast that next year's profit will be $3 million; long-term debt, $15 million; and equity, $21 million. You can figure that a drop greater than $1 million in anticipated net income would cause a default (.75 = $15 million/X; X = $20 million; necessary decline in net income = $21 million − $20 million, or $1 million). In light of that margin, you must decide how likely such earnings performance is.

A basic negotiating posture

At the outset, the banker will try to impose as many tight restrictions as possible, especially if yours is a small company or one that has traditionally dealt with one bank. Address each proposed restriction individually and push for its elimination, or at least its relaxation, by using an appropriate mix of the following arguments:

Management needs strategic flexibility to avoid default.

Even if the restriction is dropped, the banker will still achieve the objectives with the remaining covenants.

A strong balance sheet shows that company assets provide a secure, secondary source of repayment if earnings deteriorate.

A strong earnings outlook means the bank can tolerate a weaker balance sheet. Large payouts of cash are acceptable since strong future earnings make it possible to service the bank debt by refinancing.

The banker can tolerate large payouts of cash or other managerial actions because, if earnings deteriorate, a trigger covenant will be violated and the bank can then demand tighter covenants that closely control management.

Watch out for unnecessarily tight dividend restrictions or capital expenditure limits. You can have them dropped or relaxed if your balance sheet is strong enough or if you can point to a low amount of business risk. To the extent that you can, stress: (1) your high margin of safety (low leverage), the liquidity of the balance sheet (high current ratio), and the availability of your assets as a secondary source of repayment even if earnings are used for something else; and/or (2) that your strong earnings will permit a refinancing if they are used for something other than debt servicing.

A borrower with a strong balance sheet and a low level of business risk can usually convince the banker that a very loose dividend restriction (e.g., "cumulative dividends and stock repurchases shall not exceed 45% of cumulative net income") is acceptable. Or you can maintain that the debt-to-equity ratio and the current ratio (or net working capital minimum) adequately protect the bank from excessive payouts of the company's equity.

If you are not so fortunate, try to make trade-offs among covenants. For example, bankers will reduce controls on cash flow if you agree to an easily released trigger. If you start losing money, the trigger will cause a default and allow the banker to demand a tightening in the controls to stop the cash drain.

Eliminate duplication

The smart manager will insist that the banker can achieve many objectives through a single covenant. For example, the debt-equity ratio restriction can control management's use of leverage and also serve as the yardstick for a trigger if the company incurs losses.

If the banker proposes a net worth minimum as a trigger and a debt-equity ratio as a brake on leverage, the manager can argue for elimination of the trigger because the debt-equity ratio is a sufficient control. The banker may counter by maintaining that he wants to safeguard loss control directly, but the borrower may at least get the restrictions relaxed somewhat.

Relax the trigger

When a trigger is too restrictive, you may be able to show that even though future earnings might be less than planned, this would not necessarily reflect a fundamental or long-lasting deterioration in the company's earning power. In the previous example (where more than a $1 million fall in net income, from the forecast of $3 million to less than $2 million, would have violated the .75-to-1 long-term debt-equity limit), you might argue that such a profit decline could be caused by temporary factors beyond your control, such as bad weather or strikes. Or make the point that an exact forecast is impossible and you need a wide enough margin for error to properly test decisions.

You will have better luck with this appeal if you show that your company's assets will still provide an assured, secondary source of repayment if the banker relaxes the covenant from .75 to 1 to, say, 1 to 1. Prospects for strong earnings also may help you bargain for more flexibility on the use of debt financing.

Dealing with strategy control

A strategy restriction often leads corporate executives to seek a more "enlightened" bank. Unfortunately, if one bank thinks this kind of control necessary, usually most others will agree.

Rather than shopping around, find out why the banker objects to a strategy; then point out your thinking behind it and the importance of flexibility. After all, success here should guarantee future earnings power. Then agree to other restrictions—for example, a tight trigger that allows the bank to put a stop to the strategy if it results in losses. If, after considerable discussion, the bank officer continues to regard the plan as inappropriate, consider financing from a source less averse to risk than a commercial bank.

A competing note...

Some *Fortune* "1000" companies shop for the best terms by requesting several banks to bid on a loan. They instruct bidders to quote the interest rate, the compensating balance arrangement, the repayment provisions, and a set of restrictive covenants. Such a procedure—or even the *threat* of it—influences some banks to propose more acceptable terms.

I do not suggest that all companies, particularly smaller ones, use this technique. Before negotiating a term loan, however, you should obtain some information on the types of covenants that might be demanded either by visiting with financial officers in companies that have recently raised bank debt or by talking with lending officers to get a feel for the types of covenants that might be required. Armed with this knowledge, you can mention the requirements of other banks when the potential lender is unduly restrictive.

...and a concluding one

Covenants set at the time a loan is negotiated that allow you free rein still may prove restrictive in light of future opportunities. However, compliance can be—and nearly always is—waived or the covenant amended if the bank's review of a project shows it to be strategically appropriate without drastically altering the risk picture.

Appendix:
the typical bank loan agreement

Bank loan agreements contain a *representation and warranties section* normally stipulating that the borrower:	The *affirmative covenants section*, considered "boilerplate covenants," includes promises that the borrower will:	The *negative covenants section* stipulates any number of the following promises that the borrower will not:	
Is properly incorporated.	Submit annual, audited financial statements.	Permit some type of debt-to-equity ratio (e.g., total liabilities-to-equity or long-term debt-to-equity) to exceed a specified maximum.	Pledge its assets to another creditor (a variation is to pledge its assets unless the bank is equally secured by the assets).
Has the power and authority to enter into the loan agreement and the promissory note.	Submit periodic (usually quarterly or monthly) unaudited, interim financial statements.	Permit the interest coverage ratio (EBIT/interest expense) to be less than a specified minimum. (Other coverage tests are also used; *cash flow coverage: net income + depreciation/current maturities* of long-term debt shall be no less than a specified minimum.)	Merge with or acquire another company (a variation is to merge with or acquire another company unless the borrower is the surviving company and no violation of a covenant would result).
Is current on its taxes.	Submit periodic certificates signed by an officer of the company stating whether the company is in compliance with the loan agreement.		
Is not the subject of any litigation except as disclosed.			
Has good title to its assets.	Maintain its corporate existence.		Sell its assets (except inventory in the ordinary course of business and obsolete or fully depreciated equipment), unless the money received is used to retire the bank loan or to buy replacement assets.
Has not pledged any of its assets except as disclosed.	Maintain adequate insurance.	Permit additional borrowings.	
Is not in violation of any other credit agreement.	Maintain its corporate assets in good condition.	Permit guarantees of third-party obligations to exceed a specified dollar amount.	
Has made full disclosure of its financial condition in its most recently submitted financial statements.	Pay all taxes unless contested in good faith.	Permit the current ratio to fall to less than a specified minimum.	Permit investments (such as the purchase of common stock or bonds of other companies), loans, or advances to exceed a specific dollar amount outstanding.
		Permit net working capital to fall to less than a specified minimum.	
		Permit annual capital expenditures to exceed specified dollar amounts.	
		Permit dividend payments and stock repurchases to exceed a specified cumulative or annual dollar amount.	
	Occasionally a banker will tailor a restriction. For example, one institution recently prohibited an agricultural commodities trader from incurring a loss that exceeded a certain amount on closing out all long and short positions.	Loan agreements also list *events of default,* including failure to pay principal or interest when due, failure to comply with an affirmative covenant after notice of the violation has been given by the bank, violation of a negative covenant, discovery that a representation or warranty was incorrect, a default in the payment of money owed to another lender, and bankruptcy of the company.	The *remedies section* states that should a default occur, the lender may declare the entire principal of the note, together with accrued interest, immediately due and payable.

Reprint 82201

Labor Unions

Keeping Informed

What arbitrators think about technology replacing labor

Richard D. Sibbernsen

If nothing else, management is about keeping up with the times. The "times" are an ever-shifting combination of foreign and domestic competition, deregulation, and new technology. And these days, keeping up means buying and installing new equipment to ensure continued high performance. Whether the new equipment will work out, however, greatly depends on whether an efficient crew can operate it. And although it may seem a simple matter to fit the crew to the technology, it's not. What gets in the way?

In many industries, to maintain a competitive edge and survive, managers have to eliminate work rules and practices that no longer reflect operating conditions and that thereby result in serious inefficiencies. Many employers have adopted a new labor relations model that makes both opera-

Mr. Sibbernsen is senior vice president, corporate relations, for the J.I. Case Company, a Tenneco subsidiary that manufactures agricultural and construction equipment on a worldwide basis. He has held various corporate human resources and labor relations positions in Tenneco companies and represented the company in several cases discussed in this article.

tions and people more efficient. And new work structures are wiping out the decades-old, rigid manning customs and shop floor regulations that have been institutionalized through the collective bargaining forum.

The immediate payoff for management is lower break-even operating levels, increased profit margins, and greater ability to compete effectively in the global market. For employees the benefit of improved performance is better job security. These days, both employees and their representatives perceive with great clarity the relationships among competitive pressures, operational costs, and keeping their jobs.

In the steel, meat-packing, paper, and auto industries, management is aggressively cutting the size of crews and enlarging some jobs by adding duties. Executives of auto, rubber, oil refining, and paper companies are combining craft jobs such as those of millwright, welder, and boilermaker. In many industries, multiskill and broadly defined job classifications have replaced traditional production jobs. For example, whereas most auto factories have dozens of job classifications, the recently negotiated labor pact between the General Motors and Toyota joint venture and the UAW provides for four. The

agreement also allows the New United Motor Manufacturing Inc. to proceed with an efficient team approach to car assembly.

According to rubber industry experts, such work-rule changes can boost employee productivity by at least 10%. Oil refiners project that such changes have increased employee output by 15%, and one steel company claims that in five years it has cut the man-hours required to make a ton of steel from six to three and a half.

These widely publicized work structure changes fall into two categories: those that leave the existing organization of work intact but more efficient, combining jobs and eliminating unnecessary positions, and those that change the system itself, creating multicraft jobs and pay-for-skill or "team" work arrangements. This trend toward restructuring work is closely related to another change in work practices—altering job assignments.

When manning levels get improved, not everything gets better. But the conflicts with union job security claims that arise can be avoided. This shop floor revolution runs up against basic issues of union jurisdiction, job rights, and established practices and expectations.

> *"When manning levels get improved, not everything gets better. But the conflicts with union job security claims that arise can be avoided."*

Through productivity bargaining with the unions, many employers have achieved work design modifications in which each party agrees to specify well-defined work organization or manning level changes in a document.

But the obstacles to happy settlements are many. Competitive pressures and operational costs as well as the labor relations climate in operations may deny management the time and the opportunity to reach a meeting of the minds with the unions. Some employers may be unwilling to pay the price the unions request in exchange for negotiated work-rule changes—long-term employment guarantees, hefty wage payments, detailed financial disclosures, codetermination of strategic business decisions. Also, as a matter of policy, many employers, preferring to reserve the flexibility to adjust work procedures continually, won't agree to write detailed manning-level or work-rule changes.

Employers such as U.S. Steel and Inland Steel try to restructure the work and reduce operating costs by aggressively and unilaterally reducing classifications and reassigning job duties on the shop floor. The Massachusetts Bay Transportation Authority, under legislative authority allowing it to redesign the work structure and eliminate unneeded positions regardless of union objections, has reduced its work force by 10%.

In cases like these, the union often seeks protection from unilateral action by filing grievances alleging that management has violated the provisions of the parties' labor contract. Any manager wanting to streamline an organization through unilateral crew size reductions or job consolidations had better carefully review the relevant labor relations standards or risk losing a challenge in the arbitration forum.

What I'd like to do here is explore the accepted arbitral authorities that govern management's right unilaterally to initiate productivity improvement programs that involve job combinations, crew size reductions, and work restructuring. I hope the article will serve as a helpful guide to managers who are trying to establish optimal manning levels. I hope that nonunion as well as union employers can learn what operational issues are crucial to consider while reducing the work force or restructuring work methods.

Before we go on to examine management's rights and limitations, I want to review a case that illustrates how some of these issues arise.

A case in point

Let's look at a 1982 labor contract dispute and a resulting arbi-

tration award that involved the Packaging Corporation of America, a Tenneco company, and the International Printing and Graphics Communication Union. The Grand Rapids, Michigan facility in question manufactures folding paperboard cartons. It is a mature business in a very competitive market that is made up of 35 different companies operating 40 folding carton operations. The plant employs 220 hourly-rate production employees who for almost 30 years have been represented by Local 555 of the international union.

The labor contract expressly reserves to management the right to determine "the schedule of production and the methods, process, and means of production," provided "these rights are not used to violate any terms of this Agreement, nor for the purpose of discriminating against any employee." The contract also contains language that allows the union to raise a grievance regarding how the terms of the agreement are applied or interpreted.

The manufacturing process is divided among several departments. Part of the production flow requires printing presses, and the company uses two six-color offset printing machines (a 78-inch Miehle and a 60-inch Harris) that run on a continuous three-shift basis. After the printing stage, the product moves through the cutting and finishing departments and on to shipping.

After the purchase of the Harris press in 1967, management and the union negotiated a "letter of understanding" stipulating that a five-employee crew was to operate this press "with operating conditions as they currently exist." Two years later, they reached a similar understanding when they bought the Miehle press. For the next 12 years, all press operations followed these manning practices.

The dispute arose out of management's decision to restructure the work on the presses and reduce the number of employees in the crews. This was part of an across-the-board cost-reduction program spurred by declining market opportunities and increasing competitive pressures. In November 1981, management notified the union that it was going to install new equipment that would simplify the printing process and reduce the work load of the press operators.

On September 10, 1982, the production manager met with the

union representatives and announced that the new equipment wouldn't justify keeping the six-color offset press crew at its current manning level. He made a point of commenting that recently completed industrial engineering time studies verified that a reduction in personnel would not unduly increase the remaining employees' work load. Emphasizing that such action was necessary if the operation was to keep its market share, he noted that many competitors were maintaining quality, productivity, and make-ready time standards with press crews of fewer than five.

The union officials did not believe there was a need for reducing the crew sizes, and the two parties were unable to reach a meeting of the minds. At this point, consistent with its plantwide cost-reduction program, management unilaterally reorganized the presswork and reduced the crews.

The local union filed the following grievance challenging the crew reductions: "The employer has violated the understandings contained in the 1967 letter in altering the manning of the equipment in question. The Company has also violated the mutual commitments with the union as established in the modes of action, [past practices] which have become an integral part of the [bargaining] relationship. The changes in the manning have created an undue burden upon the remaining crew members, and such changes have not substantially reduced the quantity of work to be prepared by the crew members."

The parties were unable to resolve the dispute, and the local and international unions elected to arbitrate the issue. The grievance was heard by Arbitrator J.E. Jason on May 27, 1982 in Grand Rapids. At the hearing, through its brief opening statement and the oral testimony of both union officials and press crew members, the union put forth the following arguments:

☐   The 1967 letter of understanding and clear shop practices have established a binding agreement that all crew sizes are to remain the same during the term of the contract.

☐   Before initiating any job eliminations or crew reductions, management is contractually obligated to obtain agreement with the union.

Questions arbitrators ask

Contract language
Does the contract limit management's prerogative to reduce the work force as challenged? (Most arbitrators construe the scope of such prohibitions quite narrowly.)

Collective bargaining history
Has management's right to combine and eliminate jobs been the subject of prior contract negotiations, grievance settlements, or arbitration awards?

Past practice
Is there a substantial precedent for this action? Has the company combined or eliminated jobs or reduced crew sizes in the past at the involved facility? Examples of several successful or unsuccessful job combination and elimination efforts in the past will help establish the extent to which the management of a particular operation possesses proper authority to take such action.

Operational justification for the action taken
Does the challenged job structure modification result from operational changes or from lack of sufficient work in the jobs being combined? Arbitrators often search for facts demonstrating that changes in the means, methods, processes, materials, or schedules of production or that modifications in administrative procedures have reduced or eliminated available work or job

duties. Disapproval of management's action is likely if the arbitrator concludes that the duties of the previous jobs are not sufficiently diminished to justify the challenged job elimination.

Resulting work load
Do the work load changes and procedures pose an unreasonable burden or create an undue safety or health risk for employees? Although they don't always affect the outcome, the work methods studies of professional industrial engineers, industry manning surveys, and supervisory and employee testimony are relevant information.

Impact on the union or bargaining unit
Is the job change a method of discriminating against the union or unduly prejudicing the status of the bargaining unit?

Impact on each employee
Has the challenged job restructuring hurt the future employment opportunities and wage earnings of displaced employees? To ensure that an action was truly justified and not arbitrary or capricious, arbitrators closely scrutinize any job elimination that results in loss of employment or substantial reduction in earnings. The implied "fair dealing" standard requires that the arbitrator balance the equities in each case and determine the matter case by case.

☐ Although the press equipment has changed since 1967, such changes do not substantially modify the type of operation, reduce the quantity of work the crews perform, or alter the job duties.

☐ Because the issue was not raised during the recently completed negotiations, the letter of understanding that prohibits the company from initiating any crew reductions is in effect.

☐ The changes in manning levels have placed an undue and unsafe burden on the remaining crew members.

PCA's lawyers countered with these arguments:

☐ Under the language of the contract, management possesses the authority to determine the number of employees and job classifications to be assigned to a particular operation.

☐ No contract language prohibits the involved action.

☐ Operating conditions have substantially changed since 1967. Thus the letter of understanding does not constitute a prohibition on management.

☐ Industrial engineering studies and a competitive survey illustrate that management made the decision to reduce the crews in good faith and has not created a safety hazard or an undue burden for the crew members.

In making his decision, Arbitrator Jason most likely asked the questions outlined in the insert. Before seeing how Jason decided the case, however, let's go over what arbitral standards he had to refer to.

What management can & can't do

Most American arbitrators recognize that businesses possess certain management rights. Such freedoms of action, intended to efficiently and safely accomplish the goals of the enterprise, include the prerogatives to determine manning levels, combine jobs, reduce crew sizes, and assign work. These fundamental rights are considered to be reserved to management and do not evaporate merely because there is a labor agreement.[1]

Running parallel to the "reserved rights" doctrine in the American system of industrial jurisprudence is the well-established principle that an implied "covenant of good faith and fair dealing" is embodied in each contract, including labor agreements. In the course of interpreting rights under a labor agreement, arbitrators usually apply this doctrine of "implied obligations" to the extent that it establishes a boundary of reasonableness on the reserved-rights contract construction theory. Thus in resolving job consolidation and work-restructuring disputes, an arbitrator normally inquires about the operational reason behind the decision and examines the controlling labor contract provisions.[2]

What's the agreement and why change it. Management's authority to eliminate jobs and reduce manning levels unilaterally during the term of a collective bargaining agreement is a classic arbitration subject. In his *Omaha Cold Storage Terminal* award, Arbitrator J.F. Doyle succinctly summarized the basic arbitral standards governing job elimination and crew reduction decisions.[3] He concluded that decisions on this subject fall into two broad categories:

☐ One line of opinion is that wage and job classification schedules in a labor agreement have the effect of freezing such classifications for the life of the contract. Under this theory such contract provisions are proof of the parties' intention to agree on the classifications as well as the wage rates. Thus management may not add duties to or eliminate any of the enumerated classifications. In this view job classifications in a labor contract supersede a management rights clause and application of the reserved-rights doctrine.[4]

☐ The other line of thinking is that a negotiated rate structure in a labor agreement does not guarantee that any specified classifications will remain unchanged during the term of a labor contract. These arbitrators recognize that economic necessity in a competitive market makes it essential that management be able to adapt the work force to meet changing conditions.

If no contractual prohibitions exist to the contrary, arbitrators have a strong tendency to recognize the employer's right to eliminate job classifications.[5] The right to change is not, however, absolute. Management must exercise this prerogative subject to the implied contractual obligation to act reasonably and for proper objectives and purposes.[6]

For instance, here are the words of Arbitrator H.S. Block on management's duty to act reasonably: "Where arbitrators have upheld management's rights to eliminate jobs or classifications and reallocate individual job duties, they have stressed that such changes must be made in good faith and based on factors such as change in operations, technological improvements, substantially diminished production requirements, and established practices."[7]

Assuming that no restrictions exist in the language of the labor agreement, the key issue is simply whether the challenged manning reduction is a reasonable exercise of management discretion linked to legitimate operational needs. Thus arbitrators view very carefully the past dealings of the two parties in such matters and the operational "why" behind the challenged decision.

A fine example of the type of operational inquiry an arbitrator normally initiates in such cases is found in an award issued by Arbitrator T.J. Lewis. In this instance, because of a decline in production and the findings of recently completed work-measurement studies, management had eliminated a helper's classification. Arbitrator Lewis reviewed the subsequent production results, the work loads, and the employer's practices thoroughly, as he did the contract language and bargaining history of the parties. In denying the grievance, he said that the surrounding operational needs as well as the contract language supported the challenged action. These are his words:

☐ "The decision to eliminate the job was the result of a good faith judgment to reduce costs and increase production per man hour...."
☐ "While the witness for the union described the company's motivation as being 'just to save money,' that is not an illegitimate move...."
☐ "This [elimination] was accomplished without placing significant added pressures or work loads on the machine operators."[8]

Indeed, if the contrast doesn't hold prohibitions, the critical arbitral question is usually whether the company has good and sufficient reasons to support its decisions.[9] Although certain job eliminations have been deemed appropriate simply as a method of reducing costs, such action is difficult to justify in cases where the work has merely been rearranged and no substantial change in operations has occurred. In one case, the employer had argued that the classification was eliminated because the duties were no longer being performed. On close inquiry, the arbitrator found that the same duties were in fact being performed by employees in other classifications.[10]

Arbitrators have, however, held job eliminations to be proper where the principal duties or functions of the employees involved have ceased to exist because of the introduction of new equipment, technology, or work methods. In all such cases, management has been able to demonstrate that the jobs were eliminated because of radical changes in circumstances. The arbitral scrutiny focuses on whether the changes in the equipment or working conditions are material.[11]

Repeatedly, automation and the modernization of operations are seen as "good cause" for the elimination of certain jobs.[12] Some arbitrators have, however, denied grievances even in cases where no significant and demonstrable change in operations has occurred.[13]

Of course, it is up to the union to show that any job combination, job elimination, or reduction in crew size is arbitrary, unreasonable, and causative of an undue, unsafe work load for remaining employees. Usually management refutes such allegations by presenting at hearings professional work method evaluations, industrial engineering studies, industry surveys, and supervisory or employee testimony that explain the work loads and the reasonableness of the challenged actions.

Past practice and guarantees.
Although the language in contracts that stipulates management's "maintenance of working conditions" as well as manning-level practices has often been held to restrict the employer's right to determine crew sizes and eliminate jobs, such clauses and shop practices have not in all situations been held to freeze the number of employees in a crew or a job classification. If the operational basis for the traditional or guaranteed condition (current manning levels, crew sizes) is modified, such contract provisions have not been seen as restrictive. This may also be so even when the contract contains a "local practices guarantee." Arbitrators have reasoned that if new technology or processes alter the underlying operational basis from which such guarantees or practices evolve, assigning employees to suit the old custom is unnecessary.[14]

In determining whether management may unilaterally discontinue long-standing work assignment practices, the arbitrator usually explores the relationship between the practice and some given set of operational circumstances. Since management's common rationale for assigning a particular number of employees to a given crew is work load and skill levels, arbitrators uphold crew reductions when a decrease in these requirements results from capital improvements to equipment or new methods of operation.

Even though there aren't any hard-and-fast rules, the faster management begins a crew reduction or a job elimination after a change in operations, the better. Any delay suggests that the new working conditions have not sufficiently altered the foundation

Further reading

Lloyd H. Bailer,
"The Right to Assign Employees
in One Job Classification to
Jobs in Another Classification,"
*Industrial and
Labor Relations Review*,
January 1963, p. 200.

George W. Brooks,
"Unions and Technological Change,"
Conference Board Record,
June 1968, p. 46.

Ralph T. Seward,
"Arbitration and the
Functions of Management,"
*Industrial and
Labor Relations Review*,
January 1963, p. 235.

Saul Wallen,
"The Arbitration of
Work Assignment Disputes,"
*Industrial and
Labor Relations Review*,
January 1963, p. 193.

Ronald L. Wiggins,
*The Arbitration of
Industrial Engineering Disputes*
(Washington, D.C.:
Bureau of National Affairs, 1970).

of the established practice and that therefore the manning levels should not be disturbed. Under certain conditions, however, arbitrators affirm crew size reductions even though a long time has elapsed between the first of several changes and the crew reductions. In one award, even though the union had demonstrated that the crew size had become an established shop custom, the Board of Arbitrators ruled that substantial, cumulative changes instituted by the employer to overhaul the entire warehouse and shipping procedures and practices affected the basic operating conditions. The board added that changes in product mix, equipment, and work practices over several years justified the modification in that particular case.[15]

I cannot emphasize enough that in labor-management agreements in which maintenance of local working conditions is specified and well-established crewing patterns exist, the burden is on management to demonstrate convincingly that a change in work load, equipment, or other technology justifies a job elimination. When management can't prove a change in basic operations, arbitrators generally grant a grievance.[16]

But even when management can demonstrate changes in the underlying production process or working conditions, if contract clauses specify manning levels, they are binding. When one agreement stipulated that "no less than three men shall be employed on a crew," regardless of a reduction in the volume of work, technological changes, and a lighter work load, an arbitrator ruled that the employer might not reduce the crew size.[17] When the contract provision is less explicit, however, the rulings may become more uncertain, and arbitrators may narrowly apply such restrictive manning provisions.[18]

The pivotal issues are the clear contract language as well as whether the employer has modified or eliminated the basis for the crewing relationship and, if the employer has, whether the changed circumstances warrant ending the crewing relationship or a particular position.

A recent study gives a fine summary of the labor relations principles governing management's rights to take such action: "Arbitrators are in general agreement that where substantial changes in technology or manufacturing processes have been made, management has the right to make changes in the size of the crew, unless restricted by the agreement. This is true even where the contract contains a local working conditions clause, for it is reasoned that the changes in technology or practices cause a change in the basis for the existence of such conditions. Of course, the changes must be substantial enough to result in a material reduction in the employee's work load in order to justify the reduction in crew size."[19]

Typical union arguments.
The general rule arbitrators follow is that the claimant bears the burden of persuasion. In this kind of dispute, the union claims that management has violated the labor agreement between the two parties. It is for the union, therefore, to demonstrate with clear and convincing evidence that the company's action was inconsistent with either the express terms of the labor contract or with the implied covenant of reasonableness and good faith. Indeed, while challenging job combinations or eliminations, unions usually advance several general contract arguments other than violation of past practice or the creation of an unreasonable work load. Normally, they contend that contract provisions addressing seniority, wage schedule, and recognition issues affect management restrictions.

A great number of arbitration awards have, however, established the principle that clauses in collective bargaining agreements covering recognition, seniority, wages, and so forth do not per se restrict an employer's right to combine or eliminate jobs if the employer does so reasonably and in good faith.[20]

Unions often argue that wage rate and job classification schedules limit the employer's right to combine or eliminate a classification unilaterally. But as Arbitrator W. Rothchild observed, this argument has not prevailed generally, and arbitrators usually hold that though any change in wage rates must be negotiated with the union, such restrictions do not extend to the content of the jobs involved.[21]

Likewise, another arbitrator denied a challenge to management's prerogative to modify job duties. He specifically ruled that an agreement on a job title and its rate of pay cannot be considered as forever fixing the method of operation or the particular number of employees who will take on the assigned duties.[22] Such clauses are interpreted as statements that when work of a certain nature is done, management will pay a certain wage.

In addressing union charges that the seniority rights of employees implicitly limit management's right to take unilateral action in eliminating jobs, arbitrators generally hold that these rights do not do so.[23] In other cases, arbitrators have ruled that seniority claims protect certain rights but do not guarantee the continued existence of all jobs.

Although most arbitrators do not allow unions to bootstrap such wage schedules, seniority, or recognition clauses in order to prohibit such action, these clauses do form the contractual framework from which companies' implicit obligation to act fairly develops.

Meanwhile, back at the plant

If you were Arbitrator Jason, how would you have ruled on the grievance the union filed against Packaging Corporation of America? Was the company within its rights?

After scrutinizing the labor agreement and the oral testimony and documentary evidence both parties offered concerning shop practices and working conditions, Jason ruled that management had not violated the labor agreement. He found that:

☐   The management rights clause of the contract supports the validity of the reduction, and no specific contract term restricts this management action.

☐   Offered testimony and documentary evidence prove that management had good reason to reduce the crew size because of the improvements in the operating conditions of the presses. Equipment changes and technological improvements had greatly altered the work effort and skill levels required of the crew.

☐   Management affirmed the reasonableness of its actions through a time-and-motion study conducted by professional industrial engineers that demonstrates that a reduced crew can safely and efficiently operate the presses. The crew with the usual five men had an inordinate amount of idle time.

☐   PCA had thoroughly surveyed industry practices and determined that most of the competition operates similar presses with only three-man crews.

☐   In light of the evidence entered in the record that the underlying operating conditions have changed radically since the installation of the equipment and the establishment of a five-man crew standard, the 1967 letter of understanding has not been violated.

The arbitrator's ruling focused on the existence of clear contract language supporting the reduction, the absence of any contractual restrictions, and the reasonableness of PCA's actions. For its part, management demonstrated the business logic behind its decision, the impact of change on the jobs, and the contractual support for its position.

Reprint 86212

References

1 Owen Fairweather, *Practice and Procedure in Arbitration* (Washington, D.C.: Bureau of National Affairs, 1971), p. 176.

2 Ronald L. Wiggins, *The Arbitration of Industrial Engineering Disputes* (Washington, D.C.: Bureau of National Affairs, 1970).

3 Omaha Cold Storage Terminal, 48 LA 24.*

4 *Esso Standard Oil Co.*, 19 LA 569; see discussion in *Kraftco Corp.*, 61 LA 521.

5 *Marinette Paper Co.*, 30 LA 403; *Hudson Pulp and Paper Corp.*, 37 LA 7; *Mead Corp.*, 42 LA 643; *Kimberly Clark*, 34 LA 80; *Continental Can*, 35 LA 603; *National Container Corp.*, 29 LA 687; *Master Lock Co.*, 61 LA 971; *Ohio Brass Co.*, 62 LA 913; *Amoco Oil Co.*, 65 LA 577; *Continental Oil Co.*, 71 LA 185; *Lucky Stores*, 76-2 ARB 674; *Southeastern Trailways Inc.*, 78-1 ARB 3101.†

6 *Evans Products Co.*, 29 LA 677; *Carbide Power Co.*, 26 LA 780; *Goodyear Tire*, 28 LA 374; *Johnson Bronze Co.*, 34 LA 365.

7 *American Cement Corp.*, 48 LA 72.

8 *Packaging Corporation of America-Vincenes*, 78-2 ARB 8416.

9 *Mobil Chemical Corp.*, 1975 ARB 8026; *Borg-Warner Plumbing Products Div.*, 63 LA 384; *Mead Corp.*, 64 LA 421; *A.S. Abell Co.*, 66 LA 492; *Seattle-Post Intelligencer*, 66 LA 717; *Knights of Columbus*, 67 LA 334; *Kelly-Springfield Tire*, 72 LA 742; *Freeport Kaolin Co.*, 72 LA 738; *Mid-America*, 79-2 ARB 4973.

10 *Lone Star Steel*, 26 LA 10; *National Biscuit Co.*, 38 LA 799.

11 Pike and Fischer, Inc., attorneys at law, *Steel Workers Handbook on Arbitration Decisions* (Washington, D.C.: United Steel Workers of America, AFL-CIO-CLC, 1981).

12 *Kraftco Corp.*, 61 LA 517.

13 *Virginia Folding Box Co.*, 51 LA 1051; *Ruralist Press Inc.*, 51 LA 549; *Bethlehem Steel Corp.*, 61 LA 1222; *Lever Brothers*, 65 LA 1299; *Oberdorfer Foundries*, 66 LA 1069; *Certain-Teed Corp.*, 77-1 ARB 3683; *Clinchfield Coal*, 77-2 ARB 4905; *Southeastern Trailways Inc.*, 78-1 ARB 3201; *United States Steel*, 34 LA 127; *Bethlehem Cornwall Corp.*, 37 LA 319; *United States Steel*, 62-2 ARB 8676; *Pittsburgh Steel Co.*, 43 LA 771.

14 *United States Steel*, 41 LA 56.

15 *United States Steel*, 62 LA 125.

16 *Modern Bakeries*, 39 LA 939; *Wyandotte Chemicals Corp.*, 46 LA 230; *International Salt Co.*, 41 LA 1188; *Celanese Corp. of America*, 30 LA 705; *Freeport Kaolin Co.*, 72 LA 738.

17 *Weston Biscuit Co.*, 21 ARB 653.

18 *Air Reduction Chemical and Carbide Co.*, 41 LA 24; *Anheuser-Busch Inc.*, 36 LA 1289.

19 Frank Elkouri and Edna Asper Elkouri, *How Arbitration Works* (Washington, D.C.: Bureau of National Affairs, 1979), p. 473.

20 *Reynolds Metals Co.*, 25 LA 44; *Bernheim Distilling Co.*, 28 LA 441; *Buckeye Cellulose Corp.*, 76 LA 889; *Kraftco Corp.*; 61 LA 521; *Gulf-Western Industries*, 62 LA 1132; *Yale University*, 65 LA 435; *Southeastern Trailways Inc.*, 78-1 ARB 3201; *Marine Association of Chicago*, 70-1 ARB 3480.

21 *Pacific Telegraph and Telephone*, 75 LA 1117.

22 *Continental Can*, 71-1 ARB 8407.

23 *Keene Corp.*, 70-2 ARB 8712; *Packaging Corporation of America-Vincenes*, 78-2 ARB 8416.

*Vol. 48, *Labor Arbitration Reports* (Washington, D.C.: Bureau of National Affairs), p. 24. All "LA" references come from *Labor Arbitration Reports* and start with name of case and volume number and end with page number.

†*Lucky Stores*, vol. 76-2, *Labor Arbitration Awards* (Chicago: Commerce Clearing House), p. 674; *Southeastern Trailways Inc.*, vol. 78-1, *Labor Arbitration Awards* (Chicago: Commerce Clearing House), p. 3101. All "ARB" references come from *Labor Arbitration Awards* and start with name of case and volume number and end with page number.

Thinking Ahead

New labor-management models from Detroit?

Daniel D. Luria

Today's dramatic increase in global competition requires management and labor in America's basic industries to rethink the wage, benefits, and work-rule patterns that have become entrenched over the years. Pay cuts, two-tier wage plans, and narrower application of seniority have become commonplace in the auto, steel, and farm equipment industries. Industry-wide pattern compensation agreements are fading from the scene.

A new accommodation is needed to help make older companies in established industries more competitive. Otherwise, without government trade protection, aggressive companies in newly emerging nations with clear notions of what it takes to win market share in those industries will wipe out established companies that have operated under rigid labor-management arrangements.

The U.S. auto industry has been a pacesetter in both industrial relations policies and wage structures. New developments in its labor relations and investment policies are of special interest. If labor and management fail to meet the competitive challenge in the auto industry, the repercussions for the economy will be much worse than a comparable failure in another industry. New accommodations

in this sector will set new standards and patterns. These will surely become models for others. New models are, indeed, in the works in Detroit.

Because of the pressure of foreign competition, traditional wage and benefits packages, along with agreements on work rules and job classifications, are under attack everywhere in the auto industry. Foreign imports and outsourcing have severely weakened the bargaining power of the automobile unions. As a result, every plant siting decision and every sourcing change is a response to market pressures to reduce the costs of production.

Whether welcomed as dynamism or disparaged as turbulence, the reality is that capital is more mobile and profits less certain today. And the deals that management and labor cut during the 1950s and 1960s, when the Big Three automakers—General Motors, Ford, and Chrysler—and the United Auto Workers set the pattern for both large and small suppliers, are coming undone. These pressures affect U.S. small-car assembly plants and parts suppliers with special force because foreign import competition is greater in this segment than in large-car and truck assembly.

The issue is whether global market forces will overwhelm the auto

industry because of the inability of labor and management to find a new common ground. Will a productivity coalition—an alliance involving concessions from both sides and perhaps requiring a role for government as well—emerge in time to restore the auto industry's competitive edge in domestic markets?

In 1985, the Auto-in-Michigan (AIM) Project conducted interviews with nearly 100 auto industry managers and labor leaders to provide Michigan policymakers with informed projections of likely developments in several areas, including labor relations, technology, and the use of new automotive materials. My particular interest was to learn about changes in work-assignment and job-classification rules and the trend toward replacement of pattern wage bargaining by plant-specific and multiple-tier wage and benefits agreements.

We wanted not only to understand current efforts to incorporate wage and work-rule policies into a strategy of enhanced global competitiveness and survival but also to forecast the likely trend in labor relations over the next decade. To the extent that the automobile industry continues to be a bellwether of trends in other basic U.S. industries, our findings are relevant for labor relations in many manufacturing sectors.

Rules & classifications

Negotiated work rules and job classifications, which confine plant workers to certain tasks and make promotion and assignment contingent on rules like seniority, had their origin in management's desire to reduce the amount of skilled labor required in manufacturing and other tasks. Narrow definition of jobs, some of which could be assigned to less skilled workers, was management's way of reducing the

Mr. Luria is senior researcher at the Industrial Technology Institute, Ann Arbor, Michigan and director of the Auto-in-Michigan Project, a program established by the Michigan Department of Commerce and the University of Michigan to assess the impact of changes in the auto industry on Michigan through 1992.

power of the skilled crafts. Ironically, workers now use the rules and job classifications to preserve employment. The result is that unforeseen rigidities have been introduced into the organization of work.

These rules have come under increasing attack. Many in management believe these rules retard the implementation of more automated technologies; all agree that they inflate labor costs.

"Autoworkers and their UAW representatives are willing to make substantial concessions— but only if they believe management will join in a coalition aimed at improving productivity."

Although most union representatives are much less critical of these rules, even they acknowledge that many have outlived their usefulness. As a result, with the loaded gun of excess capacity aimed at their facilities, local union leaders have been willing to go along with a more flexible organization of work and fewer job classifications in many plants, including most Big Three plants. These changes have been carried out through plant-by-plant negotiations with management, often as quid pro quos for management's commitment to continue investing in U.S. plants.

As one of the people we interviewed phrased it, "Most of the horror stories have been cleaned up." Still, few labor representatives deny that many dysfunctional practices are embedded in the auto industry. During our research, we visited an assembly plant where, until 1982, the rules required six different job classifications just to move parts from the truck to the line. "God only knows how *that* ever happened. It must have been late at night—done to put an agreement to bed," one of our respondents said. Today, thanks to more flexible work rules,

one worker does all six "jobs." Though still on the books, the other five classifications are not filled.

Throughout the industry, a number of experiments have been conducted in an effort to overcome these rigidities. A number of new deals have been agreed to, including these:

☐ As recently as 1982, in General Motors' Pontiac, Michigan Plant 8 (Oldsmobile Supreme, Buick Regal), 80 of the UAW's 100 skilled trades classifications each had at least one worker. Now those 80 classifications exist mainly on paper. Only 14 of the 100 original trades groups are filled. The result? Plant workers now undertake a much broader range of duties than before. Plant 8 closed in 1982. It reopened in 1984 after workers agreed to these changes. At GM's Pontiac Plant 1 (Fiero), only 7 trades classifications are filled. This consolidation was management's condition for agreeing to put Fiero production in the plant.

☐ At Ford's Rawsonville, Michigan parts plant, management started a pilot employment guarantee program in exchange for a reduction in trades classifications. Less skilled workers may handle routine maintenance and repair, while tradesmen operate in broadly skilled teams. Under the terms of this program, workers with at least one year's seniority cannot be laid off during the life of the agreement. They are also guaranteed no fewer than 32 hours of pay each week.

☐ At Associated Spring, a Barnes Group subsidiary in Ann Arbor, Michigan, UAW members agreed to a pay freeze, less time off, and a reduction in job classifications in exchange for management's commitment to invest $1.6 million in the facility and to seek no further concessions for at least two years.

☐ International Harvester obtained the UAW's agreement to relax work rules at its four UAW-organized plants in return for a guarantee not to reduce the UAW's share of the total hours worked in the company.

☐ At Rockwell International, the UAW traded relaxed work practices and a stretched-out progression to top pay rates for a provision under which major layoffs automatically trigger higher severance pay.

☐ In 1984, GM, Ford, and Chrysler negotiated the Job Opportunity

Bank program with the UAW. Under this program, each of the Big Three contributes funds to provide income and training for workers with a year or more of seniority who lose their jobs as a result of changes in work rules, technology, or the outsourcing of parts purchases. In exchange, management gets flexibility in assigning such workers.

☐ The agreement reached between the UAW and GM for the new Saturn plant will loosen seniority rules and also dispense with job classifications. Instead, workers will be organized in work units headed by working counselors rather than foremen. These work units are largely self-managed, having only minimal department-level supervision. GM agreed to a provision that makes 80% of the Saturn work force secure against job loss except in the case of a "catastrophic event"— something left undefined in the agreement.

Although autoworkers—skilled and unskilled—now handle a broader array of assignments in many plants, the basic skilled trades boundaries generally have not been breached. The United Auto Workers' Skilled Trades Department, which oversees but cannot control negotiations over local trades classifications, has no objection to a more efficient consolidation of plant duties as long as they occur *within* a basic trade (machinists, toolmakers, and diemakers, for example, grouped together in a single category). The department has, however, strenuously objected to efforts at consolidation *across* basic trades (for example, combining the functions of electrical workers, millwrights, and diemakers. At two Chrysler plants where management is seeking more flexible worker assignment policies, the UAW is resisting because the proposed consolidation would cross basic divisions between the crafts.

Though most union representatives are sympathetic to management's concern about productivity, they believe that auto executives may be overreacting to past rigidities. Management doesn't realize that some of the proposed solutions may cause more problems than they solve. As one respondent told us, "They don't see all the downtime that will occur when untrained workers screw up repair and maintenance jobs." Several union representatives we talked with recalled the problems General Motors ran into during the 1960s in its new southern plants. When it tried to operate plants with just three trade groups (electrical, maintenance, and tooling), downtime increased on its assembly lines. GM was finally forced to add more skilled trades classifications to the plants.

Although the new automated technologies have eliminated the need for many craftsmen in routine operations, semiskilled workers simply lack the expertise to cope with major maintenance problems. Automation increases the number of craft jobs that a good handyman can do, but as one of our respondents stated, "There's no substitute for a plumber when your pipes burst."

Managers in many of the Big Three's auto-body-panel stamping plants and in the smaller suppliers' plants haven't had to negotiate trade-offs with the union. They have often obtained work and job-rule concessions simply by threatening to close down the plants. Although such threats generate great ill feeling within the work force, market pressures on the automakers' stamping plants and on the smaller independent suppliers have given management the upper hand.

The pressures for change are clearly uneven. Restrictive work rules and narrow classifications have lasted longer in those sectors of the industry that can best withstand foreign import and outsourcing competition—for example, in plants that assemble large cars and trucks or that make large-car engines, automatic transmissions, major body stampings, and axles. In the Big Three companies, workers in small-car assembly and in engine and parts plants have accepted changes in union work practices because these factories are more vulnerable to foreign imports.

Although the auto top brass likes to claim that a more flexible work-rule and job-classification policy will lower production costs enough to keep production in the United States, nobody knows precisely what the savings in labor and other costs will be. From a companywide engineering study conducted by one of the Big Three, one can infer that as much as 37% of plant downtime results from restrictive work practices, which works out to approximately $200 in added costs per vehicle. Although the union has usual-

ly defended rules either on grounds of equity (insisting on seniority because it is a neutral basis for work assignment) or quality control (requiring that maintenance jobs be done by skilled people), the traditional job-classification system can cause costly delays in production.

What the companies need to do, however, is make a more persuasive case against "restrictive" work practices. It's up to them to provide credible data on the cost of these practices. It's also important to know whether greater workplace flexibility will have more than just a marginal effect on competitiveness.

To be sure, scattered anecdotal evidence points to a relationship between a loosening of work and job rules on the one hand and lower production costs on the other. A General Motors spokesman told *Business Week* in mid-1982 that changes in work-rule and job-classification agreements had reduced hourly costs by as much as $4.50 in some plants. At one assembly plant where our research team conducted interviews, we were told that having operators clean their own work areas made it possible to reduce the number of sanitation workers from 140 to 60. According to my estimate, this saves $15 per vehicle.

In other plants, the evidence isn't as clear-cut, usually because those plants have undergone changes in more than just their work practices. At the crankshaft department of one engine plant, employment was halved and costs cut by $10 per engine. Although work rules had become more flexible, new programmable computers had also been installed at about the same time, thus complicating the task of assessing the precise contribution made by greater work-rule flexibility.

Chrysler's Sterling Heights assembly plant makes three cars per worker to every two produced per worker at General Motors' Orion plant. At full capacity, NUMMI (the GM-Toyota joint venture in California) and Mazda (when it opens in Michigan in 1987) will turn out twice as many cars per worker as Orion—and General Motors' Saturn plant may do even better than that. Clearly, reductions in work rules and job classifications are partly responsible for this greater productivity.

If and when research is finally done to assess the effect of these

changes on auto manufacturing and assembly costs, the most sizable cost reductions will probably come from the broadening of job descriptions to enable production workers to set up and maintain their own equipment. Automation should hasten this trend because it will expand production workers' tasks and also lessen the need for skilled maintenance workers on standby in case of equipment failures.

Even if greater flexibility in work practices can be shown to lower production costs, it may not be enough to offset the advantages gained from outsourcing abroad. The wide disparities between U.S. and many foreign wage and materials cost structures give companies powerful incentives to avoid meaningful trade-off agreements. Although the Big Three did trade some income security in exchange for concessions from the UAW on work rules and pay and benefits provisions, management's commitment to a deal may weaken if it judges the savings too low to regain competitiveness. As one union respondent noted, "They can build in Mexico with the same technology, *no* work rules, *and* slave wages." (Mexico, however, requires many more inspectors than do plants in the United States because U.S. plants have better quality control systems. But that may increasingly be the only advantage U.S.-based producers enjoy.)

Our findings suggest that workers in the auto industry, on balance, prefer changes in work rules to cuts in pay, when they have the choice. In many small and medium-sized parts suppliers, the complex work restrictions found in the Big Three automakers and larger independent suppliers never took root. Perhaps because unions have so little in the way of work rules to trade, they have had much more difficulty protecting workers in these companies from pay and benefits cuts.

Although workers prefer the relaxation of work rules to cuts in pay, most workers and union leaders—when given the choice—will moderate wage demands to save their jobs. Many autoworkers and almost all union representatives are genuinely interested in working with management to build a new productivity coalition because they want to stem the job shrinkage in the Big Three automakers and the major independent suppliers.

Erosion of pattern bargaining

The other big adjustment the industry is seeking to cope with rising global competition is the replacement of pattern wage and benefits bargaining with multiple tiers of pay and benefits. Although most labor representatives are understandably distressed, auto industry executives would be glad to be free of contracts that require similar wage and benefits levels for comparably situated companies in the industry and often standard pay and benefits packages for all plants of the same company.

Pattern bargaining arose after World War II when GM saw that uniform industry wages and benefits would give it a competitive advantage over Ford and Chrysler. GM set the pattern for the other major auto manufacturers with the result that between 1948 and 1979, assemblers in all UAW-organized General Motors, Ford, Chrysler, and American Motors plants earned within 3 cents an hour of each other. GM also sought a formula-based pay increase system to give it predictability in costs.

Until 1981, autoworkers received a 3% annual "improvement factor" above any increase intended to cover inflation. This GM-initiated system set the pattern not only for other automobile manufacturers but for most basic U.S. industries as well. As long as the leading companies in these industries held onto their unchallenged market positions, this system acted as a stabilizing force for the entire economy.

By the early 1950s, the Big Three's practice of pattern bargaining had also become the norm among large independent suppliers—TRW and Bendix (now Allied Automotive), for example—though pension benefit levels were often an exception. From 1980 on, however, pattern bargaining came under increasingly fierce attack.

Chrysler was the first to break away because it could no longer afford to sustain the pattern in the face of intensifying competition. It had only one small-car line in a market that was rejecting larger cars. In addition, its midsize and large-car lines were plagued with recalls.

Pattern bargaining also began to break down in the supplier companies. Management cited the unequal costs of providing similar benefits packages as one of the reasons. Companies having higher ratios of retired to active workers, for example, have correspondingly greater benefits costs. Another reason was the markedly different competitive positions these companies faced.

The result? Suppliers have negotiated wage and benefits contracts that vary widely, both among themselves and in relation to the wages and benefits the UAW negotiates with the major automakers. The UAW-Budd master agreement once covered four plants but now covers only two.

Many of the new and planned Big Three small-car plants have work practices that differ from the industry standard. They, along with some parts plants, are also likely to split off from the pay and benefits master agreements negotiated for large-car and truck assembly plants. Since 1982, the UAW-Big Three contracts have permitted certain provisions of the master national agreements to be waived if doing so would reverse a management decision to outsource.

Signs of the breakdown in pattern contracts are everywhere. In a March 1985 *Automotive News* article, a GM vice president said that future national agreements would be limited to "philosophies and those kinds of things." The 1984 Job Opportunity Bank program and the UAW-Big Three waiver provision suggest that lower labor costs in the Big Three's component manufacturing plants may be the price for maintaining a high level of vertical integration in U.S. auto production.

In Japan, in sharp contrast, there is less vertical integration, and labor costs are steeply tiered: 25% of Japanese autoworkers get the "OEM rate" (final assembly, major body stamping, and engine and transaxle assembly), while 75% get a rate that is 20% to 70% lower. In the United States, in contrast, about 50% of the value of a car is produced in companies with labor costs exceeding $20 an hour. How could Ford's Batavia, Ohio transmission plant, one of our interviewees asked, compete with Mazda when Ford's labor costs for component casting are $24 an hour whereas Mazda's are only $9 an hour?

Additional wage tiers seem inevitable in many Big Three parts plants, especially those producing trim, small hardware, bearings, and die castings. Companies making parts whose manufacture is labor-intensive or that are sold to other industries besides auto are candidates for reduced pay scales. "Multiple wage and benefits patterns are coming," one union representative told us. "But we won't let it happen randomly, a plant at a time. If bearings are a competitive problem, we'll take all the bearings plants down a notch together." Whether the UAW will adhere to that promise of uniform downscaling remains to be seen. "Whipsawing" (the practice of making plants within a company compete against each other for work) continues, with very little union resistance.

Lower pay rates at some Big Three plants would in turn depress wage ceilings among the large independent parts makers. In the past, the major automakers and large independent suppliers started a new worker at 85% of the maximum pay scale for the job. New workers got the maximum after 18 months. But supplier executives now want starting pay rates that are 50% of the maximum and a ten-year progression before workers reach top rates.

U.S. suppliers face severe competition not only from Mexico and other foreign countries but also from the newer U.S. plants built by Japanese-owned suppliers. These new plants have a labor-cost advantage of $4 to $7 an hour in comparison with older facilities, less because of wages than because of the lower pension, medical, unemployment insurance, and other benefits costs that newer plants have. Simply stated, the newer factories don't have to support as many retired and laid-off workers.

Observing that other industries are moving to two-tiered wage structures, one supplier executive told us bluntly that his company's willingness to make substantial new investments in plant and equipment would be conditioned on getting the union to agree to new-hire rates closer to $10 an hour rather than $20 an hour within five years.

Over the next five to ten years, wage and benefits negotiations are likely to include the following elements:

Exhibit   Production costs of a small-car manual transaxle

		United States	Japan	France	Korea
Part A Before the deal	Direct and indirect labor	$ 92.00	$ 34.67	$ 69.33	$ 21.60
	Materials	150.00	145.71	172.86	162.86
	Equipment amortization	71.43	54.81	89.12	74.60
	Transportation and tariff		30.00	25.00	35.00
	Total cost	**$ 313.43**	**$ 265.19**	**$ 356.31**	**$ 294.06**
	Percentage of U.S. cost	100 %	85 %	114 %	94 %
Part B After the deal	Direct and indirect labor	$ 68.00	$ 34.67	$ 69.33	$ 21.60
	Materials	145.71	145.71	172.86	162.86
	Equipment amortization	62.50	54.81	89.12	74.60
	Transportation and tariff		30.00	25.00	35.00
	Total cost	**$ 276.21**	**$ 265.19**	**$ 356.31**	**$ 294.06**
	Percentage of U.S. cost	100 %	96 %	129 %	106 %

Note:
This exhibit is based on a model developed by Richard Hervey of Sigma Associates.

☐   More contracts along the lines of the agreement the UAW reached with GM for the Saturn plant work force. Some part of the wage will be tied to profitability and perhaps to productivity.

☐   Multiple master agreements within companies. Some plants or plant types will be covered by wage and benefits contracts that differ from those covering other plants.

☐   Starting pay scales pegged at a much lower percentage of the maximum pay rate for most job classifications, with more time required to reach the maximum.

An emerging productivity coalition?

The wide disparity between auto manufacturing costs in the United States and some other countries—despite a cheaper dollar—has created powerful incentives for management to move U.S. auto production from older Frostbelt plants to lower-cost Sunbelt and foreign production facilities. The problem is not exclusively one of wage differentials; it is also a matter of differences in plant productivity and in wage and benefits tier structures.

U.S. autoworkers and their UAW representatives are primarily concerned with employment security. They are therefore willing to make substantial concessions on work rules and on pay and benefits policies in contract negotiations—but only if they believe management will join them in a coalition aimed at improving productivity and keeping investment in existing plants. Labor also wants to be certain that it won't be forced to accept severe reductions in living standards.

Is a productivity coalition between labor and management possible? If so, is it coming?

The logistics of complex production is an important factor in favor of keeping auto manufacturing jobs in the United States. For example, just-in-time production benefits from having most parts production in proximity to final assembly. Domestic political pressures and concerns, which create uncertainties for both labor and management, would also ease were the parties to develop a stable joint strategy for rejuvenating domestic manufacture.

A productivity coalition presumes not only equality between the partners but also a willingness to forgo short-term advantages in the interest of developing long-term solutions.

Will labor tolerate increasing inequalities in pay and benefits within its ranks as a quid pro quo for keeping jobs at home? Will management give labor a role in investment decisions, especially decisions affecting production siting and the level of foreign component sourcing? Involvement of labor in investment decisions reaches far beyond the kind of plant-level issues handled, for example, in quality-of-work-life programs—or even the labor role envisioned for GM's Saturn plant. Without active and broad *companywide* participation in investment decisions, workers and their union representatives will have to take the corporate commitment to employment security on faith—which is hardly a good basis for a workable productivity partnership.

Cooperation between management and labor has become a well-established practice in European societies, whether called social partnership, industrial democracy, or codetermination. Government guarantees have usually stabilized these arrangements by protecting industry from sudden marketplace shocks through the use of protectionist trade policies, subsidies, and the like.

If labor and management are to make productivity coalitions in our basic industries work, they must both agree to short-term sacrifices—more flexible work practices and perhaps lower pay as well, at least in some plants. In exchange, management must accept somewhat lower returns on investment as a result of forgoing the full exercise of its outsourcing prerogatives. But it's not clear that management will offer such deals, particularly at the supplier company level. The bargaining power of organized labor may have eroded so much that manufacturers no longer depend on union cooperation and thus feel no need to offer a productivity coalition on acceptable terms.

For the sake of argument, let's assume that management can be persuaded to agree to a deal that labor considers fair. Part A of the *Exhibit* shows the present cost differential between small-car manual transaxle manufacture in the United States and abroad. We assume that each U.S.-made transaxle requires two hours of direct labor, two hours of indirect labor, and $150 in purchased material. Also assumed are a 1,880-hour work year, equipment amortization of $50 per unit, a 5% scrap rate, and 70% machine utilization.

Part B of the *Exhibit* illustrates what would happen if labor and management agreed to a deal in which labor modified work practices in exchange for management's commitment to invest in existing transaxle facilities at home. The data in Part B assume a 15% increase in the productivity of direct labor, 80% machine utilization, a 2% scrap rate, and a ratio of indirect to direct labor of 0.7 to 1. Under this scenario, instead of losing all 850 jobs, the United States would lose only 236. In other words, 614 jobs would be saved.

The cost gap between U.S. production and low-cost foreign manufacture would fall from $48.24 to $11.02 per unit after the deal. If one assumes that the advantage of proximity to U.S. assembly plants isn't enough to offset this $11.02 cost differential, then management would still have an incentive to move more auto production offshore.

What might the remedy be? If the cost to the U.S. Treasury of losing domestic production is greater than the remaining cost gap, then selective subsidies or tariffs might be an effective way to bolster the new productivity coalitions and keep production in the United States. A government subsidy or tariff of $11.02 per transaxle would cost the U.S. Treasury $5.5 million. It would, however, preserve 614 transaxle plant jobs and perhaps 2,000 related U.S. jobs. While there is room for debate on the *costs* of protection— more expensive cars and foreign retaliation—a measure that saves high value-added industrial jobs for $2,100 each clearly looks like a bargain. Moreover, phasing out such a subsidy or tar-

iff over, say, five years would both support the productivity coalition *and* make demands on its continued vigor.

Careful thought needs to be devoted to this issue. On the one hand, we have an opportunity to build industrial strategies that may stem the accelerating decline in domestic plants' market share in our largest industries. On the other hand, increased competition from abroad has accelerated domestic companies' outsourcing, which is hardly a prescription for improved relations between management and the unions.

Consider what has been happening in the U.S. steel industry. Although some steel companies have negotiated forward-looking contracts similar to those in the auto industry, U.S. Steel's plan to buy slabs offshore may well jeopardize hopes for a progressive labor agreement with its workers.

At present, there may be no informed basis for discussing either the extent of labor cost moderation or the economic penalty to domestic production. Having a common data base and a forum to consider its implications would force both unions and managements to think more carefully, systematically, and programmatically about restructuring their industries.

Without a context in which to develop their own strategies to handle the slimming down of their industries, unions have no choice but to defend every job even if doing so costs many more. Without the need to defend their restructuring plans to labor and the public, management may rush into outsourcing and thereby impose costs on society that far outweigh the penalty for retaining domestic production. Luckily, that penalty is declining in the case of the auto industry. The strengthening of the yen against the dollar creates a window of opportunity because the competitive gap to be closed is now smaller.

Can a deal be cut? It's my belief that productivity coalitions can succeed. As I've suggested, some reasonably fair deals have already been cut between labor and management in many sectors of the U.S. automotive industry. But over the next several years, we'll need to see many more such deals if our basic industries are to achieve competitiveness without damaging our living standards and our social and political traditions. ▽

Reprint 86510

Thinking Ahead

Jack Barbash

Do we really want labor on the ropes?

We're entering a new era of industrial relations, and that's cause for concern

Most observers agree that the 1980s mark an important period in industrial relations. Agreement ends there, however, as analysts differ about the meaning of recent trends and events.

To some, the concessionary contracts of late seem only a momentary adjustment in a steadily evolving relationship between employers and unions. Others point to the spread of quality-of-work-life programs and other forms of cooperation between managers and workers and argue that industrial relations are improving. The decline of adversarialism, say these people, is a hopeful sign as American companies move toward Japanese-style management.

Yet for all the publicity given to the new cooperation, other evidence suggests that industrial relations in the United States are moving down a different path. This author, an eminent labor economist, surveys current developments and sees alarming signs that the balance of power has shifted from unions to employers. He argues that employers are mounting an aggressive campaign to overturn many of organized labor's bargaining achievements, and he poses disturbing questions about the social consequences of the unions' fall from favor.

Mr. Barbash is Bascom Professor of Economics and Industrial Relations (Emeritus) at the University of Wisconsin. He is the author of many articles and books on the American labor movement, the most recent of which is The Elements of Industrial Relations *(University of Wisconsin Press, 1984).*

In the last few years, two trends in our system of industrial relations have become apparent. First, employers have made a determined drive to get the unions to make concessions. Behind this management offensive are fundamental changes in the political economy of the United States: the decline or deregulation of unionized industries, the growing power of foreign and nonunion competitors, the accelerated movement of enterprise to the Sunbelt, and public policies designed to bring labor to heel.

Second, the unions have responded to these pressures by trying to ride out the waves of concessions, by dampening their militancy, and when possible, by bargaining for job security in return for concessions. For the longer term, the unions have been relying on a political strategy (unsuccessful in 1984) of dislodging opponents from the White House and Congress and attempting to organize employees in nonunion sectors of the economy.

In my view, these trends and events are symptoms of radical change in our system of industrial relations. By *radical,* I mean fundamental, thorough, long-term change in the relationship between labor and management as it has evolved in the United States from the Depression onward. The 1930s were a time of radical change in the same sense, although the developments then worked to labor's advantage. The radicalism of the 1980s lies in the passing of the bargaining initiative from labor to management, the shift of management's strategy from defense to attack, and the transformation of piecemeal bargaining adjustments into an entirely new relationship.

The recession that began in 1979 acted as a catalyst to force undercurrents of structural change in industrial relations to the surface. This recession was pivotal, not only because employees suffered wage and job losses but also because those losses were huge and were concentrated in smoke-stack industries and regions. In the past few years, wage and bargaining structures have been revised drastically, and the union as an institution has been facing a frontal assault. The recovery has not put an end to management's drive for concessions, nor has it slowed the pace of change. Indeed, the 1980s will be a decade of change.

Management on the offensive

Employers' tactics to push their offensive include aggressive bargaining to contain wages and benefits, the shaping of new bargaining structures, and sophisticated ways to avoid unions altogether. Some employers combine or complement these hard tactics with softer ones, such as cooperative programs between labor and management and a more straightforward approach to negotiations.

Editor's note: All references are listed at the end of the article.

Attacking labor costs.
A sharp deceleration of negotiated wage increases (or outright wage cuts), massive layoffs, and plant closings have been signal features of collective bargaining in recent years. Wages, fixed wage increases (cost-of-living adjustments and annual improvement factors), and fringe benefits, especially those in health care and pensions, have been frozen or reduced. Wage increases in major collective bargaining agreements were lower through 1984 than at any time since the Bureau of Labor Statistics began tracking them 17 years ago. Despite the recovery, wage results in 1984 continued to reflect the impact of the recession. Employment in the auto and steel industries fell by one-third from peak levels in the 1970s. Employees in the public sector have also suffered pay cuts and job losses.

Employers have focused their bargaining efforts on particular components of labor cost, including soaring health care costs, confining work rules, and the wage structure itself, whose median continues to rise as the work force ages. In attacking the health care problem, employers have pressed for both more competition from suppliers and lower rates of use by employees and their families. On the supply side, management and labor have agreed in many cases to replace a single, prescribed health care plan with a variety of competitive options, including comprehensive care at a fixed price in an HMO, the preset fee schedule of a preferred provider, and more restricted use of existing programs. On the demand side, management—this time in the face of union resistance—has pressed for employee cost sharing through deductibles and coinsurance.

The elimination or reform of work rules has been a prime target of management's offensive. Employers claim that these rules get in the way of a company's ability to adapt quickly to changing competitive conditions. Management's aim is to foster maneuverability on the shop floor by broadening job classifications, which would allow employees to move easily from job to job, permit flexible scheduling, remove barriers to subcontracting (perhaps with nonunion subcontractors), and eliminate fixed manning requirements. In a few instances, employers have dislodged the old rule structure with an entirely new work system built around teams and job rotation.

Creating new structures.
Some employers have negotiated changes in basic features of our system of collective bargaining. For example, a two-tier wage structure, one for established employees and another for new hires, is a direct challenge to the traditional union principle of equal pay for equal work. Current employees avoid large wage cuts, but a newly hired worker may earn $4 to $5 less per hour than a worker with the requisite seniority who does the same job. In the past few years, the auto, aerospace, trucking, copper, airline, and newspaper industries and the U.S. Postal Service have adopted two-tier systems of one form or another.

Employers have also tried to limit fixed wage obligations. Before the 1980s, profit-sharing agreements were not unknown in collective bargaining but they were rare. Now, profit sharing and its close relative, employee stock ownership, have become part of a deliberate policy to replace (insofar as possible) fixed obligations with performance-related and market-sensitive forms of compensation. However, the unions have largely succeeded in preserving COLA, at least in principle. Only the airlines and retail food unions have surrendered it altogether. In most other cases, the principle remains intact, but unions have accepted deferrals or modified formulas for determining the COLA.

Finally, employers have attempted to tie union wages to pay for comparable skills in the outside labor market and to avoid industrywide pattern bargaining agreements. In 1984, an arbitration panel accepted the U.S. Postal Service's argument that union wages were too high relative to pay for comparable skills in the national labor market. In the coal, steel, meat-packing, and retail trade industries, management has succeeded in negotiating separate compensation agreements on a company-by-company or even a plant-by-plant basis. The pattern agreements of the past, insists management, sheltered excessively high wages from competition and blunted market pressures on labor costs. In today's competitive environment, say employers, pattern agreements can be a severe handicap.

Avoiding the unions. A common belief among today's managers is that employees will not want a union if management does its job properly. This view contrasts sharply with positions that prevailed a few decades ago. Nearly 30 years ago, I wrote that "many tough bargainers [among employers] prefer the union to a situation where there is no union" because dealing with a responsible union is better than dealing with a disorganized mass.[1] Most companies in the rubber, basic steel, and auto industries, I then thought, fell into that category.

Employers' attitudes have changed, according to one prominent spokesman, because unions haven't lived up to their end of the bargain. They have not delivered wage protection from low-wage competition here and abroad, nor have they resisted the unrealistic wage expectations of their own memberships. Finally, runs this argument, unions complicate personnel administration by imposing and enforcing rigid rules. For all these reasons, not only do "those who hate unions" practice overt antiunionism but so do "those who have concluded in the most dispassionate of ways that living without a union is a sound business decision."[2]

Union displacement and avoidance have become realistic options for employers in the transportation, meat-packing, retail food, coal-mining, and construction industries. Employers' success depends on their ability and nerve to take a long strike and keep a business operating, to replace striking workers, and to survive union retaliation. In 1983, using tactics that a *Wall Street Journal* reporter called "old-fashioned strikebreaking," Greyhound hired replacements for 12,000 drivers on strike (65,000 people applied for these jobs) and protected them with wire fences and armed guards.[3] Phelps Dodge Corporation called on striking miners to cross their own union's picket lines. Iowa Beef Processing (now a subsidiary of Occidental Petroleum Corporation) announced that it would endure long strikes if necessary to cut wage costs—and it has done so.

In addition, antiunionism is now more openly discussed among employers. Antiunion consultants package campaigns to decertify unions and to defeat union-organizing drives. Some consultants even advise clients to goad employees into strikes if the outcome is likely to weaken the union. The American Management Association is one among many sponsors of seminars on "preventive labor relations." Participants are instructed "how to recognize and resist organizing early" and "how to make unions unnecessary in your company."[4]

A credible union avoidance strategy requires more than simply defeating an organizing drive. It also requires compensatory policies or a substitute mechanism to perform the functions that a union carries out. In the short term, at least, policies to substitute for a union can be as costly as dealing with one—or even more so. Management "buys off" the employee's union impulse, often at a premium.

The recent growth of human resource departments may really conceal a union substitution strategy in some companies. In this variant, management blunts the effects of union appeals by establishing an employment policy that is competitive with union standards and by strengthening the employee's ties to the company through systematic communication and motivation programs.

The current political climate in the United States, moreover, has emboldened antiunion employers. The Reagan administration has distanced itself from organized labor much more than its predecessors did. Since 1981, federal agencies have used their rule-making powers to modify occupational health and safety and labor relations laws. In other cases, the government has chosen not to enforce the laws. Finally, the administration has appointed persons unsympathetic with the unions to key positions in the Department of Labor, NLRB, OSHA, EEOC, and other agencies. The current chairman of NLRB, for instance, has written that "collective bargaining frequently means labor monopoly, the destruction of individual freedom, and the destruction of the marketplace as the mechanism for determining the value of labor."[5]

Two recent landmark cases in the public sector illustrate the government's position and support the new management offensive. The administration's swift and unyielding response to the 1981 strike by the Professional Air Traffic Controllers' Organization (PATCO) in 1981 not only ended the stoppage but also finished off the union. In the U.S. Postal Service, a Reagan-appointed majority on the governing board and the active involvement of an attorney known in union circles as a union buster stiffened management's resolve to join battle with its unions, an action almost unprecedented in the federal services. Despite rising productivity and an overall budget surplus, the U.S. Postal Service management justified its demands for a three-year freeze on wages, benefits, and COLA as well as a two-tier wage system on the ground that employees were overpaid by the standard of the outside labor market.

Like the Department of Transportation in the controllers' strike and employers in the private sector, postal management resorted to tough rhetoric. Postmaster General William F. Bolger announced that he would fire any employees who chose to strike. The fate of PATCO is a specter that haunts many negotiations in the federal service.

The new cooperation. As a counterpoint—or as a complement—to their hard lines, some managements have undertaken an assortment of programs to foster employee and, rather less often, union cooperation. The main purpose of these programs is to encourage a spirit of collaboration and problem solving on the shop floor, of which Japanese efforts are often cited as good models.

Trade unionists in the United States have always understood, at least intuitively, that collective bargaining depends on management and employees sharing an interest in their companies' survival. The unionists are aware that employees and their unions are secure only if their companies are solvent. Most of the time, however, unions have been willing to make concessions only when companies have been on the brink of disaster.

The new cooperation between employees and management differs from the traditional sort of cooperation in several ways. To begin with, the cooperation is intended to be continuous rather than reserved for emergencies. Second, the parties often seem self-consciously cooperative since they work together in formal programs or projects. Third, the cooperation is meant not only to improve the quality of work life (QWL) but also to reduce costs. Although the connection has yet to be proved definitively, managers assume that cooperation improves performance. Finally, some managements regard cooperation as a device to wean employees from their unions.

Cooperation of this kind generally surfaces during periods of economic hardship. Indeed, hard times may be the essential condition of cooperation. In good times, union leaders generally practice "distributive bargaining"—slicing up and apportioning the economic pie.[6] The atmosphere of crisis makes people consider forbearance and sacrifice in a new light.

In short, the new cooperation, says Brian Freeman, a union adviser, "isn't a social revolution; it's a deal."[7] Quality circles in the United States take their cue from Japanese methods of quality control. Companies proffer union representation on corporate boards to take the sting out of layoffs and wage cuts. Stock ownership and profit sharing are gaining acceptance as future compensation in lieu of present wage cuts. Employee ownership is usually a last resort to stave off bankruptcy.

The future of the new cooperation depends in part on whether certain inherent contradictions can be resolved. In participative programs such as QWL, quality circles, and employee involvement, managers and union officials have to wrestle with such questions as:

> Can cooperation survive job cutbacks, plant closings, and close supervision of the bottom line?
>
> Do employees feel motivated to raise productivity if it means fewer jobs in the future?
>
> Will employee stock ownership and employee representation on the board benefit operations and performance?
>
> How can the management and employees maintain their new cooperation in good times?

Workable answers to these questions have yet to appear. The new era of cooperation, a product of economic hardship, is simply too young to suggest a definite direction for the future.

A new bargaining mood. Related to the new cooperation–and also born of economic necessity–is a new mood of conciliation and problem solving in collective bargaining. In the long run, this mood could be vastly more important than more structured forms of cooperation. The fresh bargaining spirit appears most dramatically in the auto industry, where other forms of cooperation are also prominent. Just as auto negotiations were the vanguard of progress for other industries and unions in labor's glory days, so now are auto negotiations pacesetters during labor's decline.

The commitment to problem solving and the bargainers' disposition to avoid the usual theatrics are at the core of the new spirit. The auto negotiators are facing squarely up to the question of how to reconcile the often incompatible aims of management for efficiency with those of labor for security.

The 1984 negotiations moved toward this reconciliation by giving management a wage increase it could live with, the operating flexibility to shift employees from job to job, and the freedom to subcontract or outsource with union consultation. An income guarantee and employment (but not job) security gives the United Automobile Workers the security it demanded. Retraining and relocation are also part of the income guarantee. The New Business Venture Development Group, jointly administered by the automakers and the UAW, is an entirely new form of cooperation and falls in an area far out of the range of the employment interests of the typical union.

In other industries the new mood is reflected in the basic elements of the bargaining relationship. For example, the United Mine Workers (UMW) recently negotiated a 40-month contract with the coal operators that was the first agreement since 1966 settled without a national strike. But the new bargaining mood is still a fledgling phenomenon. And again, adversity is the driving force behind getting bargainers to negotiate with boldness and imagination.

Labor's defense

Organized labor has responded to management's offensive through active participation in politics, bargaining to protect members' economic and employment security, and organizing workers in nonunion sectors of the economy.

Campaigning in politics. The AFL-CIO's much publicized efforts to defeat President Reagan in 1984 were central to labor's efforts to regain the advantage. Having "their man" in the White House has given management the confidence to take on the unions, in much the same way that President Franklin D. Roosevelt fortified union morale by taking on the auto and steel industries a half century ago.

Given events such as the PATCO strike and the unsympathetic appointments to key federal agencies, the labor federation saw the need to campaign aggressively for the president's defeat. Reaganomics, said Lane Kirkland, former president of the AFL-CIO, is "class warfare against the disadvantaged, the poor, and the working people of America."[8]

The federation also endorsed Walter Mondale's candidacy before the Democratic primaries to minimize the dissipation of resources through internal rivalries. Mondale met the unions' specifications for a candidate to oppose Reagan: he was an experienced leader from the center of the Democratic party. Back in 1982 and 1983, when the federation was working out its strategy, Mondale seemed the strongest alternative to Reagan.

Throughout the presidential campaign in 1984, the AFL-CIO tried to persuade its members to vote for Mondale in the primaries and the general election. In the process, the unions became almost a labor subparty within the national Democratic party. In consequence, Mondale acquired a "special interests" label. Although AFL-CIO members were perhaps 20% more likely than the general electorate to support the Mondale-Ferraro ticket, they could not overcome the president's popularity and the effects of a booming recovery.

Now that President Reagan has been reelected, the labor movement faces a hard choice. It may call off the feud with the administration or it may press for sympathetic appointments in labor agencies and moderation of the Reagan hard line. Since the conservatives will be in office for at least another three years, runs this logic, a truce may be sensible. The recent appointment of Bill Brock as secretary of labor to replace the controversial Raymond Donovan suggests that the administration is taking a conciliatory tack.

The alternative would be to turn away from politics, as the AFL once did, on the theory that the law that has helped the movement can now hurt it–as the journey from the Wagner Act to Taft-Hartley to Landrum-Griffin to Reagan-era enforcement policies suggests. This jibes with Lane Kirkland's recent comment that unions may find it more effective to take on employers directly than to face the frustrations of working with the present NLRB.

Labor's political strategy is most likely to concentrate on congressional lobbying. The unions' legislative program is aimed at shoring up points of vulnerability in bargaining and at revitalizing the industrial heartland. Two issues stand out in this program.

First, an AFL-CIO industrial policy would modernize smokestack industries in the regions of labor's traditional strength. The federation proposes a tripartite social compact among management, labor, and government, a lending institution like the Reconstruction Finance Corporation of the New Deal era, and credit and tax policies to support modernization of basic industries.

Second, the unions are urging protectionism, which they say is necessary in view of the policies of our trading partners. Labor's ability to win job security in the steel and auto industries partly depends on adequate protection of domestic markets to allow employers to offer secure employment. High on the trade union agenda, therefore, are import quotas on steel and domestic content legislation to guarantee that a minimum percentage of automobiles sold in the United States will be produced here.

Bargaining for security. In collective bargaining, U.S. unions are as militant as the economic fortunes of their industries allow. With the decline of many unionized industries, labor's aggressiveness as measured by strike numbers has waned. The years 1981 and 1982 recorded the lowest number of strikes and workers involved and the lowest percentage of working time lost since the 1940s. In 1983, the number of workers involved in strikes of a thousand employees or more and the amount of working time lost just about doubled the levels of 1982.[9] But even these figures are well below the average level of the postwar years.

Direct action and protests against management have come more often from local insurgents than from national union leaders. In the most publicized case, steelworkers and church leaders in the Monongahela Valley "invade[d] Pittsburgh's wealthiest parishes, sometimes loudly disrupting the Sunday services, other times standing in silent vigil before the congregation" to dramatize the hardships plant closings have wrought.[10]

With the effectiveness of the strike weapon diminished, the unions have been attempting to cope with the economic crisis by negotiation. Many unions have extracted quid pro quos for concessions made to employers. These trade-offs included job security protections such as provision for retraining, income and job guarantees, limitations on plant closings, and restrictions on outsourcing.

The unions have also negotiated forms of contingent compensation, such as profit-sharing agreements, employee stock ownership, contract reopeners, and provisions for the eventual reimbursement of lost wages. Moreover, labor has insisted on "equality of sacrifice"—that is, on the concessions of managers and exempt employees who had been shielded from the effects of downturns and a say in corporate decisions affecting employment through union membership on boards of directors or through QWL programs on the shop floor. A pension strategy, still in its infancy, would bring investments into the service of the unions' social goals without impairing rates of return, security, liquidity, and diversification.

Organizing new territory.

U.S. unions have mounted major organizing drives in the Sunbelt with campaigns in the Atlanta, Houston, and Los Angeles labor markets. Through joint organizing agreements among the Coalition of Union Women, the Communications Workers of America (CWA), the Industrial Union Department of the AFL-CIO, and the Service Employees, the unions are also attempting to organize female clerical workers, the mass production workers of the service economy.

Other major drives are in progress to organize hospitals and nursing homes and Japanese auto plants in the United States. Some older unions such as the CWA and the UAW are attempting to organize employees in the public sector as well as nonunion industries to recoup losses in their core businesses. To date, however, none of these drives has yielded major success, except in exposure.

Finally, some unions are pursuing a corporate campaign strategy that lines up a coalition of bankers, directors, consumers, creditors, and regulatory agencies to pressure targeted companies to recognize a union. The textbook case of this strategy is the conclusion of labor actions at J.P. Stevens in 1983 after a 20-year struggle.

Putting labor's house in order. Adversity has forced some unions to reexamine their internal administration and affairs. The Service Employees and the CWA have redesigned their structures to match those of changing management organizations. The UMW is restoring responsibility for collective bargaining to the national officers after a decade of chaotic decentralization. Small unions are turning to mergers with other unions to increase their ability to weather hard times.

The AFL-CIO is working at communicating a clear image of itself to its rank-and-file constituents. Surveys have revealed that its members know that they belong to a local and an international organization but that few know exactly what the federation does. To parry Reagan's taunt that the union leadership has been out of touch with the rank-and-file (40% of union households rejected the federation's advice in 1980 to vote for Jimmy Carter), the AFL-CIO organized Solidarity Day in 1982. This event brought out a half million unionists to Washington to protest the administration's policies. In 1984 Lane Kirkland hit the hustings for the Mondale-Ferraro ticket as no previous federation president had ever done during a presidential campaign. In the process, many unionists heard of Kirkland and, for that matter, of the AFL-CIO for the first time.

The new hard line

Several decades of slowly softening industrial relations have in the 1980s given way to the new hard line of employers. The soft strategy had been to get employee consent through persuasion and to negotiate while coming to terms with greater union bargaining power. The hard strategy coerces consent by a show of market power and the threat of unemployment. This coercion is why the 1980s represent a new era in industrial relations.

Some perceive the unions' misfortunes as a sign of a bleak future. But the recession has not, as they say, "broken the backs of the big industrial unions," nor are the unions "dead," "doomed," "irrelevant," or "extinct." Such predictions and assertions ignore the essential function that unions play in modern industrial society. This role is so essential, in fact, that employers are forced to simulate unionlike structures in the unions' absence. And, while they clearly face troubled times, unions in the United States still represent nearly 20 million workers. Such institutions aren't easily broken, doomed, made irrelevant, or rendered extinct.

Antiunionism in the United States. A critical question that management's new hard line raises is why employers here formally recognize unions but, virtually alone among managements in the Western industrial world, persist in their campaign of attrition against the unions. The labor movement in Western Europe has shared with ours the experience of victimization, violence, and struggle, but once unions there proved their right to exist, employers accepted them.

The founders of our system of industrial relations confidently predicted that once the Wagner Act established the rules of collective bargaining, employers would eventually see the superiority of collective negotiations to individual relationships. In their eyes, unfair labor practices would slowly disappear, leaving only questions of administration and representation.

In the postwar period, the emergence of professional labor relations specialists within management seemed to reflect a softer view toward unions. The era of good feeling reached its height in the Kennedy-Johnson years, just before the economy confronted the full brunt of Japanese and European imports. The professionalization of industrial relations management now seems a double-edged sword with the rise of a new generation of human resource managers helping to carve out a brave new nonunion world.

The unfair labor practices of employers have continued to mount. Union victories in representation disputes have declined. Defeats outnumber victories. Labor law has been unable to moderate management's determined opposition.

Employers here are unlike their European counterparts in several ways. For one thing, Europeans recognize class differences and believe that industrial and social peace will come from recognition of employers' and employees' interests through effective representation. Americans, on the other hand, reject the idea of class, and the notion that employees need a union to protect them from their employers has always struck managers as un-American.

Now, European employers may also be more sympathetic to unions because they have not dealt with the full impact of an active union presence on the shop floor. The law regulates the employment relationship in Europe. In many countries, the terms of employment are standardized and extended throughout a region, even to businesses that are not direct parties to formal bargaining agreements. As a result, European managers have greater control on the shop floor than managers in the United States. The paradox is that ideologically conservative American unions have penetrated more deeply into management rights than have anticapitalist European unions.

The costs of labor's decline.
The European entente cordiale between employers and unions may have

been less cordial in recent years, but it is hardly conceivable that a union-free environment could ever arise as a serious alternative in Western Europe. Yet the spirit of antiunionism runs strong among employers in the United States. The issue extends beyond labor costs to the sense that somehow the unions don't belong. This attitude leaves us with disturbing questions for the future of industrial relations in the United States:

☐   Since trade unions have contributed to the stability of democratic societies throughout the West, will labor's decline in the United States unsettle that equilibrium?

☐   Will the benign aspects of human resource management continue in the absence of organized labor's countervailing power?

☐   Will public regulation fill the vacuum created by labor's decline? If so, employers' strategic choices will not be between unions and a union-free environment but between collective bargaining and public regulation.

☐   Will massive layoffs, plant closings, and wage cuts create a backlash if labor market conditions tilt again in favor of employees?

On the whole, the post-1930 strategy of "if you can't beat 'em, join 'em" has served employers well. The shock effect of collective bargaining has honed management's professionalism to a sharp edge. The contrary strategy of operating without unions may have short-run benefits but may aggravate class conflict for the long run.

Modern trade unions in the United States, unlike employee representation groups of the early twentieth century, are a powerful political and economic movement capable of effective resistance to hostile employers. A return to open struggle between management and organized labor would be detrimental for American business and for the national interest as well. The new realism of American unions, it seems to me, offers a more promising foundation on which to build the next era of industrial relations.

Reprint 85402

References

1 Jack Barbash,
Practice of Unionism
(New York: Harper & Row, 1956),
p. 210.

2 Peter J. Pestillo,
"Learning to Live Without a Union,"
*Proceedings of the Industrial
Relations Research Association*
(Madison, Wis.: Industrial Relations
Research Association, 1979),
p. 234.

3 Ralph E. Winter,
"Even Profitable Firms Press Workers
to Take Permanent Pay Cuts,"
Wall Street Journal, March 6, 1984.

4 American Management Association,
"The Non-Union Employer: Preventive
Labor Relations," course prospectus
(New York: American Management
Association, 1980).

5 Seth King,
"New Tone and Tilt on Labor Board,"
New York Times, February 2, 1984.

6 Richard E. Walton and Robert B. McKersie,
A Behavioral Theory of Labor Negotiations
(New York: McGraw-Hill, 1965).

7 Richard Koenig,
"Conrail,"
Wall Street Journal,
February 14, 1984.

8 Lane Kirkland,
"Reagan's Class Warfare,"
AFL-CIO News, July 27, 1983, p. 7.

9 "Work Stoppages Data,"
Monthly Labor Review,
March 1984, p. 103.

10 Mark Potts,
"Angry Steelworkers Extend Protest
to Some Pittsburgh-Area Churches,"
Washington Post, May 20, 1984.

Special Report

*Barbara Reisman and
Lance Compa*

The case for adversarial unions

*A traditional
labor-management
relationship,
rather than one based
on concessions
and cooperation,
is best
for both sides*

Are you inclined to the view that a new era in labor-management relations is dawning in America? Do you see trade-offs, power sharing, and cooperation replacing old-style economic bargaining and adversarialism?

Look again, say Barbara Reisman and Lance Compa. The "new era" is not in the best interests of labor or management. Furthermore, it's not really new: 60 years ago, pundits proclaimed the end of adversarialism, a call that has reemerged in each generation. But labor-management cooperation has never worked in America, nor say the authors, will it. It is simply not a part of the American industrial experience. In fact, today's cooperation is not always what it seems to be. Frequently, what is called cooperation is a disguised effort to bust the union.

Instead of pursuing this course, managers and workers should accept a well-tempered adversarial relationship. The two sides have fundamentally different interests: healthy conflict is organic to the system. Neither top managers nor labor leaders should be taken in by the current talk

of cooperation. It is far better that they stick to their own side of the bargaining table to work out differences.

Ms. Reisman and Mr. Compa both have extensive experience in the labor movement, and have served as members of bargaining committees with large and small employers. Ms. Reisman, a 1976 Harvard Business School MBA, worked for eight years in New York for the United Electrical, Radio and Machine Workers of America, including two years as research director. She is currently director of finance for the Environmental Defense Fund.

Mr. Compa joined the staff of the United Electrical, Radio and Machine Workers of America in 1973 after graduating from Yale Law School. He worked as an organizer for five years in New England and the South and is currently the union's Washington, D.C. and Baltimore area representative.

According to many academics and analysts, U.S. labor-management relations are undergoing a fundamental change: traditional adversarialism is giving way to concessions from labor and a new cooperative relationship between the two sides. These observers see the twin shocks of non-union competition in this country and low-cost, high-quality imports from abroad as forcing unions to look more favorably—and even with some measure of sympathy—at a variety of company demands: the need for wage restraint, reduced benefits, and abolition of "rigid" work rules, seniority rights, and job classifications. Under this new set of understandings, wages will be linked more directly to increases in productivity. Rather than pursue the pattern-bargained, industrywide agreements of the past, labor and management will increasingly negotiate contracts tailored to the needs of an individual company.

The most sophisticated proponents of these new developments cast their observations in a prolabor light. In return for concessions, they point out, some unions have bargained for profit sharing, retraining rights, and job security guarantees. Unions can trade give-backs for more say on the shop floor, where techniques such as quality circles, quality-of-work-life programs, and other approaches promise workers greater control over their own jobs.

Unions may even win a voice in investment and pricing strategy, plant location, and other major corporate policy decisions previously reserved to management. Advocates of trade-offs between economic concessions and such "power sharing" have pointed to the Eastern Airlines agreement, in which employees took an 18% pay cut but gained 25% of the company's stock, the right to seats on the company's board of directors, and the right to review important corporate moves before they are made. Summing up the argument in favor of this new era of labor-management cooperation, Harvard Business School Professor D. Quinn Mills writes, "Union officials must be made part of a broadened management team....If [managers] realize

Editor's note: All references are listed at the end of the article.

what is occurring and try to strengthen joint labor-management efforts to build sound businesses, concession bargaining can make a long-term contribution to the U.S. economy."[1]

We disagree. From our perspective as day-to-day participants in the real world of labor-management relations, we see concessions and all that go with them as both a costly mistake for workers and organized labor and a false signal to managers and companies. Though it is true that give-backs have been accelerating since the late 1970s — according to government statistics, nearly one-third of all workers covered by major collective bargaining agreements took a wage freeze or cut in 1983 and the first nine months of 1984 — we believe that American workers and their unions will come out of this experience with renewed commitment to their traditional adversarial role.

Our view is that this "new" era of cooperation is, in fact, nothing new at all. Rather, it is a false hope that has been seized on from time to time in the past but has never panned out. It has not worked in this country, largely because it is not part of the American industrial experience. It does not represent what workers want and need or even what managers should expect in the way of responsible unionism.

Further, proponents of labor-management cooperation today simply misread the real political and economic forces at work in this country: the agenda of the Reagan administration and numerous corporations is not cooperation but union busting. In fact, managers are unfairly blaming unions and unionized workers for mistakes of their own that have eroded their companies' competitiveness. All too often, after managers have covered these mistakes with demands for concessions, their next step is to close the plant or move the enterprise, despite workers' sacrifices.

Finally, we believe that a healthy adversarialism, with both sides representing their interests on opposite sides of the bargaining table, is a far better way for both labor and management to go. In spite of the current flirtation with labor-management cooperation, managers who formulate policy counting on a permanent new pliability in the unions that represent their employees will find themselves stumbling. So will union leaders who oversell concessions as the solution to their members' problems.

Rhetoric of the past?

In listening to our case for adversarial unions and against concessions and cooperation, critics may claim to hear the hoary rhetoric of the past — perhaps even the last gasp of a dying labor movement. Concessions and cooperation, they would say, are the only ways for unions to survive.

In fact, *their* argument is the old one. Pundits of every age think that theirs is a new era of labor-management cooperation. They concede that in the past a tough brand of trade unionism was needed to establish organized labor. But, they insist, modern times call for unions to elevate themselves above crass "pork chop" issues and give up the old adversarial relationship. As one prominent labor observer declared: "Organized labor in the United States has gone through three cycles.... The first was the period when class consciousness was being aroused.... The second was the defensive struggle for the principle of collective bargaining, a period of warfare....[Today] the third cycle lies in constructive development towards a system of cooperation rather than war."[2]

That was written in 1924, during the New Capitalism fad. The promoters of labor-management cooperation in those days touted such initiatives as the B&O Plan (in which workers exchanged economic concessions for promises of job security and participation in management), employee stock ownership of the Philadelphia Rapid Transit Company, and the investment of union health and welfare funds in the Great Northern Railroad.

These measures were evidence of a "Higher Strategy of Labor," which unions were pressed to adopt as their new approach to collective bargaining. Indeed, many union leaders saw it as their salvation. The executive council of the American Federation of Labor was moved to pronounce, "At no time in its history has the trade union had greater influence in industrial circles. The constructive policies which we advocate and follow challenge the attention and respect of employers in this country and abroad....Those who look to the trade union movement for leadership are increasing."[3] That was in 1928.

What has changed in 60 years? Today, we hear that labor-management cooperation and the trade-off between concessions and job security represent a revolution in collective bargaining. Employee stock ownership plans and other forms of employee buyouts are heralded as the answer to plant closings. Union control over pension fund investments will presumably revive the economies of the heavily unionized areas of the country. *New Republic* calls recent concession-filled settlements at Eastern Airlines and Xerox "constructive industrial bargains that simultaneously benefit labor, industry, and the wider society" and asks, "Can labor move to this higher ground?"[4]

Through the looking glass. All this rhetoric is hauntingly familiar. The New Capitalism of the 1920s proposed to make industrial conflict obsolete through a new spirit of cooperation in the workplace. Labor-management cooperation would guarantee productivity. Productivity would guarantee profits. Profits would guarantee jobs and rising wages. Workers could then buy stock, and the unjust division of society into capitalists and laborers would be overcome, replaced by a single family of owner-operators. Unions could help their members reach this grand goal, not by adversarialism, but by making the success of the company their paramount task. Those unions that stood in the way by clinging to adversarialism were dinosaurs doomed to extinction.

Variations on these themes have ranged over the years from welfare capitalism and people's capitalism to pension fund socialism and the latest pronouncements on labor-management cooperation. Taken together, they amount to a kind of through-the-looking-glass Marxism, positing a classless society of owners. Workers need only realize that enlightened managers, unlike the bosses of the bad old days, now have their best interests at heart. Similarly, according to this view, managers must see that by making union leaders part of the management team, labor will come to accept joint responsibility for the success of the business.

Unfortunately, just as the philosophizing of the 1920s proved unrealistic, so today's calls for cooperation are out of touch with political and economic realities. The Reagan administration in its first term signaled its approval of union busting when it fired the air traffic controllers and eliminated their union. Decisions by the National Labor Relations Board and the federal courts have given management license to weaken and destroy unions.

Companies may now transfer work from unionized to nonunionized locations without bargaining. They can seek to abrogate negotiated labor agreements by filing for bankruptcy under Chapter 11 of the federal law. They may initiate interrogations of union supporters in organizing campaigns. They have a freer hand to fire organizers who protest safety hazards or who are charged with minor misconduct. By committing massive unfair labor practices in the early stages of an organizing campaign so that the union is unable to sign up a majority of the employees, they can avoid ever having to recognize a union. All these developments are products of the first four years of the Reagan administration. What labor policy can unions and workers expect from an administration that called for nonunion performers at its second inauguration?

The same agenda applies in the economic environment, where proponents of cooperation overlook both the record of the 1920s and the actions of many companies today. In the 1920s, while enthusiasts promoted the New Capitalism and its cooperative labor-management ventures, most employers were busy practicing something else: the "American Plan," a blueprint to destroy trade unions by means of the open shop, the yellow dog contract, the blacklist, and the company union.

Today, merit shop, union-free environment, concessions, and labor-management cooperation are the business bywords. In our view, the real corporate agenda calls for breaking union strength by derailing union-organizing campaigns in never-organized industries or facilities, by eliminating vulnerable unions by decertification, by moving to nonunion areas of the United States and abroad, and by using the lure of cooperation to hold down wages and benefits where the union cannot be dislodged.

Advocates of cooperative relations should consider events at Continental Airlines; Phelps-Dodge's Arizona copper mines; McDonnell-Douglas's Long Beach, California aircraft center; Magic Chef's Cleveland, Tennessee appliance plant; and Greyhound Bus Lines. In 1983 and 1984, workers at these locations put up stubborn but unsuccessful resistance to company demands for concessions. They ended up taking concessions, not because of any new spirit of cooperation or in exchange for stock ownership, profit sharing, or employee involvement programs, but because they had no choice. The companies had committed themselves to breaking the unions – and were willing to hire entirely new work forces to do so. With millions of unemployed people desperate for work, management had superior bargaining power and brutally exercised it.

Those nationally publicized strikes hardly exhaust the list of union strike defeats. Moreover, many companies are taking full advantage of their bargaining edge to force union members into submission without strikes. In recent years, major concession contracts were accepted by unions in the rubber, steel, auto, trucking, and airline industries. The prospect of job loss, like that of being hanged in a fortnight, concentrates the mind wonderfully. Management's mailed fist, not the velvet glove of labor-management cooperation, has convinced millions of workers that concessions are necessary.

Who is to blame?

Gradually, however, as management's demands for concessions have spread, workers have learned that they are being unfairly blamed for management's own failures and that agreeing to concessions is no guarantee that their sacrifices will be rewarded. It is now a widely accepted view – certainly in academic circles and increasingly among executives themselves – that the blame for falling productivity and reduced competitiveness rests with management, not with union contracts.

Managing their way.... By their refusal to upgrade established plants, their compulsion to grow by merger and acquisition rather than by building their core businesses, and their obsession with short-term profits rather than long-term growth, American bosses have worked themselves into uncompetitive positions. None of these fundamental failures is the fault of American workers or their unions. As a United Auto Workers ad hoc group called Locals Opposed to Concessions said, "It wasn't our wages or benefits that caused the industry's problem in the first place. It was management – the bean counters – that made bad decisions, bad investments."

Not only are give-backs a bad-faith attempt to blame workers for problems they never caused, but the evidence indicates that concessions make little difference in management decisions. Often management pushes for concessions when there is no economic justification: a 1982 survey found that in management's own opinion fully 40% of company demands for concessions were unsupported by economic need.[5] Companies were simply out to get a piece of the concessions action. Here are some examples:

☐ Firestone Tire & Rubber Company and Goodyear Tire & Rubber extracted a series of concessions from the United Rubber Workers as a condition of continued operation at the industry's historic center, Akron, Ohio. Then they shut down major facilities anyway.

☐ The International Union of Electronics and Electrical Workers and local government officials in Yonkers, New York made contract and tax concessions in exchange for promises by United Technologies Corporation that its Otis Elevator subsidiary would remain open there. The plant is now closed.

☐ In 1983, United Auto Workers members at a Ford assembly plant outside Chicago turned down a "lifetime employment" offer tied to concession demands. Now they are being pushed for all the overtime they can work.

☐ A series of give-backs at U.S. Steel's South Works in Chicago, Illinois – based on company assurances that the concessions guaranteed new investment and job protection – concluded with the company announcing the plant's shutdown.

☐ Following store closings in Michigan and Ohio, Kroger Company officials admitted that "there isn't any [concessions] package that had a hope of being accepted that would have made the stores competitive." Conversely, the company demanded concessions in West Virginia with the threat of store closings but agreed to a concession-free contract when the union balked.

☐ In 1982, International Harvester accepted a $6.9 million federal loan, promising to keep open its Memphis, Tennessee farm equipment plant in exchange for union concessions. Concessions were given, but late last year the company announced its "nonreversible" decision to shut the plant.

☐ Eastern's 1984 experiment in labor-management cooperation, which traded concessions for employee stock ownership and the promise of a say in the business, ended in bitter recrimination when the company unilaterally extended the deep wage cuts into 1985.

The value of adversarialism. In our view, concessions do not save jobs. They just prolong the agony of dying plants and finance runaway moves that the employers would have made anyway. Companies make investment decisions to fit their strategic plans and their profit objectives. Labor costs are usually just a small factor in the equation. Unrestrained by either loyalty to their work force or political or legislative constraints on their mobility, the companies cut and run, concessions or no concessions, and then blame it on the unions.

The argument against high wages for workers should be turned on its head: high union wages underlay much of the success of U.S. industry in this century. High wages gave workers the buying power to propel the economy forward. A long-standing principle, shared by both management and labor, was that workers should earn wages that would give them the income they needed to buy what they made. If union leaders today willingly engage in concession bargaining on the false grounds that labor costs are the source of a company's problem, they lock themselves into a logic of competition with Third World pay levels – one they cannot win.

Should that continue to happen, through pay cuts, two-tier wage systems, and proposals for subminimum wages for young workers, America's social structure would indeed move toward that of a less developed nation: a small group of wealthy investors, a sizable but still minority bloc of elite professionals and highly skilled employees, and a huge mass of marginal workers and poor people.

We do not believe that American workers will comply with a continuing cycle of concessionary contracts. Under these circumstances, asking the labor movement to give up its adversarial role is asking it to collaborate in its own demise. It seems that each generation of workers must learn anew that there is no easy solution to labor problems. American workers have moved their unions forward in spurts, not at a steady velocity. The unrelenting political and economic attack on workers and unions may bring forth a new outpouring of class-conscious, aggressive trade unionism. This cannot happen, however, if unions succumb to the latest blandishments for concessions and cooperation.

The seeds of organization are taking root now with incipient organizing committees among high-tech, service, and clerical workers and in other sectors of the economy that many see as impossible to organize. In the organized sectors, we can testify to a rising mood among the rank and file to fight back against concessions and collaboration. These trends suggest that the demise of the labor movement is no more imminent today than it was before.

If, however, the labor movement gives up its tradition of independence and struggle, the new sectors will never be organized and established unions will fade into irrelevance. Only those unions with a fighting spirit and a winning record will organize the unorganized and rebuild union strength. New unions may be formed. As this fight develops, only those labor leaders and managers who have not been taken in by the "new era" ballyhoo will be equipped to understand it and arrive at coherent labor-management policies.

Those in both camps who banked on a new era of concessions and cooperation will get no return on their investment. The fact is that in the real world of American labor-management relations, managers and workers inevi-

tably come back to an adversarial position. Whether this is good or bad is beside the point; what is important is to understand why it happens.

Roots of American unions

It is neither an accident of history nor a conscious choice that the most deeply rooted traditions of the American labor movement reflect independence from employer influence, skepticism about management's motives, disdain of company unions, and toughness in the struggle to improve wages and working conditions. Employers have always sought to transform unions into instruments of management policy. Union leaders have often started down that road with management.

But rank-and-file pressure always stops them short. American workers have learned from hard experience over the years to guard the independence and militancy of their unions, particularly in a society that regards the collective nature of trade unionism as an assault on traditional property rights and the dominant individualist culture.

Union resistance to management pressure is at the heart of the employment relationship. Management *always* seeks to squeeze out more production at lower cost and to exert greater control over the work force. We intend no moral judgment of management. The logic of productivity and profitability impels managers to those ends.

At the same time, most workers want to do a good job, feel a sense of accomplishment in their work, and be recognized for it. But they will inevitably resist company pressure for ever greater physical effort, tighter discipline, and lower wages. Workers have a basic need to stick to a fair day's work, preserve a degree of personal space on the job, and improve their standard of living. Between the two sides there are certainly some overlapping interests: both labor and management can agree that diligence, discipline, and good wages are important to attract and keep a good work force. Both can agree that the survival of the enterprise is important.

There are nevertheless inherent conflicts between labor and management that run much deeper than these surface-level agreements. The workers want the enterprise to survive so that they can keep their jobs. But in management's view, it is not the company's function to provide jobs. To management, a rapidly rising productivity rate means improving profits; to workers, it means the loss of jobs. To management, an increasingly tough standard of discipline means improving profits; to workers, it means the workplace can become more like a prison than a shop or an office. To management, a declining cost from reduced wages and benefits means improving profits; to workers, it means a declining standard of living.

Since individual resistance to company pressures is futile, workers will naturally organize a collective response. They may not form a union immediately; yet managers in non-union companies know that their employees find many ways to come together. Ultimately, however, workers discover that only a union provides an ongoing means of resistance to management pressures.

Organic adversarialism.
The adversarial character of American labor-management relations is organic to an economic system propelled by hard-driving managers seeking to maximize profits. In the face of this pressure, organizing creates a new set of bonds among workers, a sense of "sticking together." Thoughtful managers understand this and recognize that union bonds do not necessarily break legitimate bonds between employees and employers.

To ask workers to loosen their bonds to the union and tighten those to the company under the rubric of labor-management cooperation is to ask them to break faith with one another. Their union solidarity is all that lets them say to their employer: "This far and no farther." Workers who exchange solidarity for concessions and cooperation violate the core of unionism and forsake the last shred of their independence—that which keeps them from becoming cogs in the corporate machine.

Many companies today recognize this dilemma. They have developed benign methods to increase production, discipline workers, control labor costs, and, at the same time, avoid union organization. These companies realize that better machinery, more rational material flows, better planning, an emphasis on "the carrot" in the workplace, and an ear to what workers are thinking will do more for production and discipline than a heavy-handed speedup.

But given the relentless pressure to improve performance, we do not believe that management can forever keep workers mollified and immune to union sentiment. In some industries unionization may take decades, as it did in the mass production industries in the early part of this century. But sooner or later, most companies will overreach. They will move from the benign to the ruthless in pursuit of more production and profit, either through wage cuts, speedups, automation, or a combination of the three.

This process applies not only to the traditional assembly line. The same principle holds for clerical work, service occupations, and even the "laid-back" world of California's Silicon Valley plants, with their employee gyms and Friday afternoon beer parties. Millions of clerical workers who monotonously process insurance claims, clear checks, type reports, make flight reservations, and stare into their video display terminals all day are subject to rigid monitoring of their output and face strict discipline if they fail to meet quotas. Health care workers see jobs being eliminated and face increased patient loads as hospitals scramble to adjust to lowered federal Medicare reimbursements under the government's new prospective payment system. In Silicon Valley, hourly workers confront assembly line demands and health hazards equal to those in smokestack industries.

A cultural revolution? Both the historical roots of American unionism and the underlying pressures that drive management suggest that those who recommend a new spirit of labor-management cooperation are asking for a cultural revolution that has no basis in our industrial reality. They are calling for the "Japanization" of the American labor movement: unions that would meet with management and then return to their members to communicate and enforce management's policies.

Such a system flies in the face of history and the real desires of the rank-and-file American worker. American workers want unions that will meet with their members in a democratic setting, listen to their needs and desires, and then approach management to press for their demands. The failure of some unions to do these things points more to a need for internal reforms than to a need to scrap the best traditions of the American labor movement. For that matter, many Japanese workers are now beginning to demand more aggressiveness and less compliance from their own unions.

However far they stray from their founding principles, unions are forged from the needs and aspirations of their members. The bedrock reason for organizing continues to be the worker's need for "somebody to back me up." American workers want an adversarial union, if they want a union at all. There is simply no other reason to have one.

Most important, we regard the notion of adversarialism as positive, not pejorative. Of course, an adversarial union is not the same as one that indulges in name calling or is strike happy. There is plenty of room for give-and-take in solving shop problems, in improving quality and productivity, and in meeting employees' needs.

But even these objectives are best achieved by having labor and management on opposite sides of the negotiating table, where both sides are conscious of their inherent differences and respectful of the other's interests and where the strength of each side serves to check the reach of the other. The compromises resulting from such a relationship may leave nobody happy—least of all the advocates of labor-management cooperation. But those compromises beat anything that could be accomplished by having both labor and management on the same side of the table.

The rocky reality

What can managers draw from our case for adversarial unions?

First, do not mistake a short-term trend for a new era or destiny. The attempts to weaken existing unions coupled with concerted campaigns to keep unorganized plants "union free"—far more prevalent features of today's labor relations than quality-of-work-life programs or "power sharing"—may succeed in some industries in the short run. Companies may make some short-term gains from two-tiered wage structures and concession agreements.

But in the long run, workers will organize to defend their jobs and improve their working conditions. If the existing unions cannot help them accomplish these goals, workers will find other approaches and methods. And if companies concern themselves only with the short-term results of their individual enterprises and fail to take into account the economic and social consequences of their actions, they may find themselves operating in an economy that cannot afford their products.

We suggest that companies pay attention to what appears to be an insatiable appetite for concessions. Companies that are truly interested in having participation from their work force, in producing a high-quality, competitive product, and in creating a work environment that encourages employee initiative and commitment can do this through the union, which, after all, has been chosen by the workers to represent them.

Quality-of-work-life teams, joint productivity committees, and similar programs that are held out as evidence of a sea change in industrial relations invariably come up against the rocky reality of labor-management conflict. A quality circle is an "unstable organizational structure that is likely to self-destruct," observe Edward E. Lawler III and Susan A. Mohrman in a recent HBR article.[6] Such programs are best understood as improvisations with naturally short life cycles. Anticipating this, managers can operate without offering workers illusory gains that produce a sense of betrayal when they find that cooperation brings them no return.

Union leaders should draw similar conclusions. First, unions that want to organize the unorganized defeat themselves by embracing concessions and labor-management cooperation. Antiunion consultants' most effective propaganda in organizing campaigns today is an account of the union's concessions record. "Join the union and join the pay-cut parade," say the management broadsides in the days leading up to a National Labor Relations Board election.

In union shops, leaders with a reputation for endorsing concession bargaining and labor-management cooperation will eventually face rebellion from their members. In personal terms, such a reputation can mean defeat for elected officers. More deeply, it can undermine support for the union by feeding the view that leaders of the company and union are in bed together. Eventually, workers in shops where union leaders go too far down the cooperation road will look for new leaders or a new union. What will happen in a few years, for example, when a majority of union members is on the bottom side of a two-tier wage structure?

We are not saying that labor leaders should never compromise. Even the most militant union leader knows that compromise is the essence of collective bargaining. Sometimes concessions are unavoidable. Moreover, responsible union leaders cannot spend all their time railing against management. They need to have a decent—if adversarial—relationship with their management counterparts in order to solve their members' problems.

But rather than cheerleading proposals for labor-management cooperation, union officers should push for economic advances and shop-floor autonomy. Instead of sugarcoating an unavoidable concessions contract with talk of a new era, they should teach their members about the economic and political forces that boxed them into concessions and about the need for economic strategies and political reforms to lead them out of the box. If union leaders take this approach, they may risk their titles as labor statesmen. But they will be closer to the fundamental values and needs of their rank-and-file members and better able to represent and defend their real interests.

Reprint 85313

References

1 D. Quinn Mills,
"When Employees Make Concessions,"
HBR May-June 1983, p. 103.

2 Warren S. Stone,
"Labor's Chain of Banks,"
World's Work,
November 1924, p. 50.

3 Quoted in
James O. Morris,
Conflict Within the AFL
(Ithaca, N.Y.:
Cornell University Press, 1958), p. 83.

4 Bob Kuttner,
"Can Labor Lead?"
New Republic,
March 12, 1984, p. 24.

5 *Business Week*/Harris Poll,
"A Management Split Over
Labor Relations,"
June 14, 1982, p. 19.

6 Edward E. Lawler III and
Susan A. Mohrman,
"Quality Circles After the Fad,"
HBR January-February 1985, p. 64.

Negotiation in the
Global Marketplace

WHO IS THEM?

by Robert B. Reich

"We" are seated at a negotiating table. "They" are seated across from us. The outcome of these talks will shape America's future competitiveness and economic well-being. But "us" is not necessarily companies based in the United States. "Them" is not foreign nations. Rather, us is the people – most prominently, the work force – of the United States. And them is the growing cadre of global managers – supranational corporate players, whose allegiance is

> ▌ In the global enterprise, the bonds between "us" and "them" are rapidly eroding.

to enhanced worldwide corporate performance, not to any one nation's economic success.

Unlike their preglobal predecessors, global managers feel little allegiance to us. In the global enterprise, the bonds between company and country – between them and us – are rapidly eroding. Instead, we are witnessing the creation of a purer form of capitalism, practiced globally by managers who are more distant, more economically driven – in essence more coldly rational in their decisions, having shed the old affiliations with people and place.

Today corporate decisions about production and location are driven by the dictates of global competi-

tion, not by national allegiance. Witness IBM's recent decision to transfer 120 executives and the headquarters of its $10 billion per year communications business to Europe, a move that is partly symbolic – a recognition that globalization must take companies beyond their old borders – and partly practical – an opportunity for IBM to capitalize on the expected growth in the European market.

As this and countless other examples show, business competition today is not between nations. Nor do trade flows between nations accurately keep score of which companies are gaining the lead. For the past two decades, U.S. businesses have maintained their shares of world markets even as *America* has lost its lead.

Nor does a nation's wealth turn on the profitability of corporations in which its citizens own a majority of shares. Cross-border ownership is booming: Americans are buying into global companies based in Europe and East Asia; Europeans and Asians are buying into companies based in the United States.

Robert B. Reich teaches political economy and management at the John F. Kennedy School of Government, Harvard University. His article, "Who Is Us?" appeared in the January-February 1990 issue of HBR. His newest book is The Work of Nations: Preparing Ourselves for 21st-Century Capitalism, *to be published in late March by Alfred A. Knopf.*

And most corporate profits are plowed back into new investments spread around the world.

Ultimately, our wealth and well-being depend on the value that the world places on the work we do, on our skills and insights. Hence the importance of the negotiations between us and them about what jobs we are to perform in the new global economy.

In this regard, the logic of the global manager is clear: to undertake activities anywhere around the world that will maximize the performance of the company, enlarge its market share, and boost the price of its stock. Our logic is just as clear: to get global managers to site good jobs in the United States. Our best interests are served by making it easy, attractive, and productive for them to do so, regardless of the nationality of the company they represent. At the same time, we need to structure the talks between us and them over the kinds of jobs they put here in a way that represents and secures our interests.

The Logic of the Global Manager

The image out of the past is a compelling one. A strong and proud American company is centered in an American community and is run by American managers. The offices, the factories, the community all bear the unmistakable mark of connectedness. But it is an image that is fading, an ideal that is more in our memories than in reality. Gone is the company town, the huge local labor force, the monolithic factory, and the giant vertically integrated corporation that dominated the entire region. Gone is the tight connection between the company, its community, even its country. Vanishing too are the paternalistic corporate heads who used to feel a sense of responsibility for their local community. Emerging in their place is the new global manager, driven by the irrefutable logic of global capitalism to seek higher profits, enhanced market leadership, and improved stock price. The playing field is the world.

This is not to impugn the patriotism of those Americans (or Italians or Germans) who manage globally. In their private lives, global managers are no doubt one of "us": no less patriotic, no less concerned about their countries' futures, no less involved in civic causes or social issues. But it is in business that global managers become "them." Their outlook is cosmopolitan – corporate citizens of the world, wherever they conduct their business. As one top IBM manager told a reporter, "IBM has to be concerned with the competitiveness and well-being of any country or region that is a major source of IBM revenue."

When it comes to global managers, no group of citizens, no government, has a special claim. Edzard Reuter, chairman of Daimler-Benz and one of the most powerful men in German industry, insists that

> **When it comes to global managers, no group of citizens or government has a special claim.**

the company has no special duty to invest in the former East Germany. "We are not national or nationalistic pioneers, but entrepreneurs," he has said. "When [there are good returns] in East Germany, we will invest. But not to do some politician a favor."

Regardless of the manager's national background, the principles are the same. The emerging global manager invests in the most promising opportunities and abandons or sells off underperforming assets – no matter how long they have been part of the corporate family or where they may be located. "You can't be bound emotionally to any particular asset," Martin S. Davis, chairman and CEO of Paramount Communications, told a reporter. Charles (Mike) Harper, head of ConAgra, the giant food-processing and commodity-trading company, which is crucial to the economy of Omaha, Nebraska, recently threatened to move the company unless the state changed its tax code. The bonds of loyalty could slip over the weekend, Harper warned: "Some Friday night, we turn out the lights – click, click, click – back up the trucks, and be gone by Monday morning."

While the tone of such a statement may sound menacing, in fact Harper's logic is anything but sinister. The new global manager's job is to exploit the opportunities created by the high-powered technologies of worldwide communication and transportation and by the relaxation of national controls over cross-border flows of capital. The global manager efficiently deploys capital all around the world, seeking the highest returns for shareholders or partners. Competition is intense and growing. The global manager who fails to take advantage of global opportunities will lose profits and market share to global managers who do.

In deciding where around the world to do what, the global manager seeks to meet the needs of customers worldwide for the highest value at the least cost. Some production will be done under the company's direct supervision; much will be outsourced. Often design and marketing activities will be sited close to the markets to be served; research and complex engineering, where skilled scientists and engineers can be found; routine fabrication and assembly, where workers are available at lowest cost. But there are exceptions – depending on products, markets, and circumstances. When there is danger that a market might be closed to imports, production might be shifted there. When two or more locations are about the same, the decision will be based on where the global manager can secure the most profitable deal.

The global manager's task is to put it all together, worldwide. For example, Mazda's newest sportscar, the MX-5 Miata, was designed in California, financed from Tokyo and New York, its prototype was created in Worthing, England, and it was assembled in Michigan and Mexico using advanced electronic components invented in New Jersey and fabricated in Japan. Saatchi and Saatchi's recent television advertising campaign for Miller Lite Beer was conceived in Britain, shot on location in Canada, dubbed in Britain and the United States, and edited in New York. An Intel microprocessor was designed in California and financed in the United States and Germany, containing dynamic random-access memories fabricated in South Korea. Chevrolet's best-selling Geo Metro was designed in Japan and built in Canada at a factory managed by Japan's Suzuki. Boeing's next airliner will be designed in Washington state and Japan and assembled in Seattle, with tail cones from Canada, special tail sections from China and Italy, and engines from Great Britain.

The logic of the global manager is not confined to large, well-established global companies. In 1989, in the first six months of its cosmopolitan life, the tiny Momenta Corporation, headquartered in Mountain View, California with 28 employees, had raised almost $13 million from Taiwanese and American investors. A small band of U.S. engineers was designing Momenta's advanced computer; the components would be engineered and produced in Japan; the actual product would be assembled in Taiwan and Singapore. Kamran Elahian, Momenta's Iranian-born founder, said to a reporter that global financing was "one of the only ways we [could] be assured of the $40 million we needed," and global production was required to "make use of the best technology that is available to the company." Switzerland's Logitech, the world's leading supplier of the "point and click" mouse for personal computers, relies on just 20 Swiss and Italian engineers, 520 technicians and marketing specialists in California, and 350 production workers in Ireland and Taiwan. Weng Kok Siew, president of Singapore Technologies, another upstart, has described his

> **Headquarters for the new global web can be a suite of rooms in an office park.**

worldwide strategy in words that could stand as the global manager's credo: "We plan to manufacture in any country in the world where there is an advantage – to make things in Thailand where the cost is low, in Germany because the market is big, to do R&D in Boston."

As competition globalizes, so must the vision of the manager. The dictates of capitalism are clear: the

The global manager's task is to put it all together, worldwide.

global manager gains profits and captures markets by putting worldwide resources to their most efficient uses.

The Logic of the Global Web

If the company town, a relic of the 1950s, is vanishing, so too is the old multinational corporation disappearing, a reminder of the 1960s and 1970s. Like the company town, the multinational exuded a sense of hierarchy, place, and order. World headquarters was, very simply, both in the center and at the top of the worldwide corporate pyramid. The location of the headquarters was a reflection of company history (the founder had begun the company in this place) or of industry requirements (headquarters had to be where the biggest factory was located or where the research and engineering was done). Managers in worldwide headquarters made all the crucial decisions, of course. Foreign subsidiaries were just that – *subsidiary* to headquarters. Their work usually consisted of exporting materials and components back to the parent corporation for assembling and finishing or of selling the parent's finished products in a foreign market. The lines of power, of communication, of corporate decision making and corporate governance all led back to headquarters.

The Fading Significance of World Headquarters. The emerging global manager works within a global web, which operates according to a new and different logic. The location of headquarters is not a matter of great importance; it is not even necessarily in the country where most of the company's shareholders or employees are. Headquarters for the new global web can even be a suite of rooms in an office park near an international airport – a communications center where many of the web's threads intersect.

In 1988, for example, when RJR Nabisco moved its worldwide headquarters to Atlanta, Georgia from Winston-Salem, North Carolina – where, years before, it had built the city's largest skyscraper, created a community arts center, and been the chief patron of Wake Forest University – the citizens of Atlanta were expecting great things. But the new worldwide headquarters turned out to be leased space in a suburban mall, housing only 450 executives and staff (about a third of 1% of the company's worldwide work force). Ross Johnson, then RJR-Nabisco's president, cautioned Atlantans to expect no more from the business than they would from any tiny 450-person company in their midst.

In fact, the global web may have several worldwide headquarters, depending on where certain markets or technologies are. Britain's APV, a maker of food-processing equipment, has a different lead country for each of its worldwide businesses. Hewlett-Packard recently moved the headquarters of its personal computer business to Grenoble, France. Siemens A.G., Germany's electronics colossus, is relocating its medical electronics division headquarters from Germany to Chicago, Illinois. Honda is planning to move the worldwide headquarters for its power-products division to Atlanta, Georgia. ABB Asea Brown Boveri, the European electrical-engineering giant based in Zurich, Switzerland, groups its thousands of products and services into 50 or so business areas (BAs). Each BA is run by a leadership team with global responsibility for crafting business strategy, selecting product-development priorities, and allocating production among countries. None of the BA teams work out of the Zurich headquarters; they are distributed around the world. Leadership for power transformers is based in Germany, electric drives are in Finland, process automation is in the United States. (For more on ABB, see "The Logic of Global Business: An Interview with ABB's Percy Barnevik" in this issue.)

The global web's highest value-added activities – its most advanced R&D, most sophisticated engineering and design, most complex fabrication – need not be in the nation where most of the company's shareholders and executives are. Ford's state-of-the-art engine factory is in Chihuahua, Mexico, where skilled Mexican engineers and technicians produce more than 1,000 engines per day with quality equal to the best in the world. Texas Instruments is fabricating some of its most complex wafers in Japan at its Sendai facility and is building an R&D center in Japan's science city of Tsukuba. Other recently or

> **Whirlpool International's management committee is made up of six people from six different nations.**

soon-to-be opened research labs in Japan: Procter & Gamble's technical center on Rokko Island in Kōbe; Ciba-Geigy's facility in Takarazuka; and Carrier Corporation's engineering center in Shizuoka prefecture. By 1990, Hewlett-Packard's German researchers were making significant strides in fiber-optic technologies; its Australian researchers, in computer-aided engineering software; its Singaporean researchers, in laser printers.

A recent study of where U.S.- and European-based global corporations site their high value-added activities confirms the trend. There was little evidence of any bias in favor of the headquarters nation, except in companies that had only recently become multinational and had not yet had an opportunity to site their high value-added activities abroad. Among more advanced companies working to spin their global webs, the tendency is to site high value-added activities all over the world.[1]

The Cosmopolitan Management Team. Increasingly, the managers who inhabit the global web come from many different nations. Take, for example, Whirlpool's approach to going global in the white-goods business. Headquartered in Benton Harbor, Michigan, Whirlpool recently formed a joint venture with the Major Appliance Division of Philips, headquartered in Eindhoven, Holland. The administrative headquarters of this U.S.-Dutch joint venture – Whirlpool International – is in Comerio, Italy, where it is managed by a Swede. On the six-person management committee sit managers from Sweden, Holland, Italy, the United States, and Belgium, with a German to be named later. Such cosmopolitanism is equally apparent at the top of the world's leading companies: IBM prides itself on having five different nationalities represented among its highest ranking officers, and three among its outside directors. Four nationalities are represented on Unilever's board; three on the board of Shell Oil. Sony has attempted to address the global team in a characteristically compact fashion: recently named as president and chief operating officer of Sony America was Ron Sommer, who was born in Israel, raised in Austria, and carries a German passport.

The threads of the new global web extend, as well, across the old boundaries of the company to include transactions between global managers in different companies. Investment decisions travel through far-reaching relationships between global companies headquartered on opposite sides of the world. Profit-sharing agreements, strategic alliances, joint ventures, licensing agreements, and supply arrangements tie together units and subunits. In the 1980s, for instance, Corning Glass abandoned its national pyramidlike organization in favor of a global web, giving it the capability to make optical cable through its European partner, Siemens A.G., and medical equipment with Ciba-Geigy. In 1990, these kinds of foreign alliances generated almost half of Corning's earnings. AT&T has also sought to transform itself from a self-sufficient bureaucratic mo-

nopoly into a multilateral global web: Japan's NEC helps AT&T supply and market memory chips; Dutch-owned Philips helps AT&T make and market telecommunications switching equipment and application-specific integrated circuits; Mitsui helps it with value-added networks.

No nation or continent is immune to the logic of the global web. In the 1950s and 1960s, for example, Europe sought to create and nurture "national champion" companies in key industries as a way to shelter domestic businesses from the onslaught of U.S. multinationals. Today these same champions are transforming into global webs with no particular connection to their own countries: France's Renault has teamed up with Sweden's Volvo to create Europe's fourth-largest industrial group; Daimler-Benz, Germany's largest industrial group, is discussing a wide assortment of links with Mitsubishi; Fujitsu, Japan's largest computer company, has acquired Britain's ICL; Pilkington, Britain's largest glassmaker, has joined with France's Saint-Gobain and Japan's Nippon Sheet Glass; Italy's Olivetti is distributing mainframe computers for Hitachi and developing laptops with Japan's YE Data.

The Japanese Exception? If there is one country that is criticized for not playing by these emerging global rules, it is Japan. But the logic of the global

> **The Japanese will be forced to comply over time or pay a stiff penalty.**

web is so powerful that the Japanese will either be forced to comply over time or else face a stiff penalty from the marketplace, the talent pool, and competitors and governments. For example, in the competition for global talent, corporations that are reluctant to consider foreign nationals for top managerial positions will lose out: the most talented people simply will not join an organization that holds out no promise of promotion. Japanese-owned companies that have been notoriously slow to open their top executive ranks to non-Japanese will operate at a competitive disadvantage.

Similarly, Japanese companies that have traditionally done most of their highest value-added work in Japan now must reconsider the economic and political advisability of this strategy. Indeed, there is evidence suggesting that the leading Japanese companies – those that are already the most international – are beginning to change. Many of the companies that were the earliest to recognize the need to establish manufacturing facilities in

1. John Cantwell, Technological Innovation and Multinational Corporations (Oxford: Basil Blackwell, 1989).

Europe and the United States are now investing in R&D laboratories and complex fabrication facilities outside Japan. By 1990, more than 500 U.S. scientists and engineers worked for Honda in Torrance, California; another 200 worked in Ohio. At Mazda's new $23 million R&D center in Irvine, California, hundreds of U.S. designers and engineers are undertaking long-term automotive research. Nissan employs 400 U.S. engineers at its engineering center in Plymouth, Michigan; Toyota employs 140 at its technical research center in Ann Arbor. Fujitsu is now constructing an $80 million telecommunications plant and research center in Texas. NEC has opened a research laboratory in Princeton, New Jersey.

Japanese investment in Europe has also skyrocketed. According to the Bank of Japan, direct investment in the 12 European Community countries totaled $14 billion in 1989 and grew by a factor of eight between 1985 and 1989, even faster than in the United States. And much of this new investment is at the high value-added end. Fujitsu, for example, has established an R&D center in Britain for semiconductors used in communications equipment; Hitachi, a British R&D laboratory for telecommunications switching equipment.

As the Japanese experience shows, to be successful globally, the global manager cannot bias investment decisions in favor of the corporation's home base. Even the appearance of bias is likely to cause political problems for the company in less favored nations – making it more difficult for the global manager to utilize the people, capital, technology, and natural resources across the global web. Successful global competitors like IBM, GE, McDonald's, Ford, Shell, Philips, Sony, NCR, Unilever, The News Corporation, and Procter & Gamble have willingly shed their national identities and become loyal corporate citizens wherever they do business around the world – siting high value-added activities in many nations, hiring foreign nationals for senior positions, and giving local and regional managers substantial discretion. As a result, these companies are usually treated by governments around the world on an equal footing with locally based companies.

By contrast, the worldwide operations of multinational giants like NEC, Fujitsu, and Mitsubishi, and even some European-based companies like Siemens, are still considered to be *foreign* subsidiaries – subunits whose identities derive from the nation where their worldwide headquarters are. As a result, these companies sometimes have difficulty gaining equal treatment with locally based companies. In fact, even the most cosmopolitan Japanese companies are finding that the general reputation of Japanese business for putting Japan's interests first is creating a competitive disadvantage, making it increasingly difficult for these companies to export their products or undertake foreign investment around the world without encountering political opposition.

Furthermore, the well-known predilection of Japanese companies to do business with each other and in a way that uniquely benefits Japan has created a backlash among corporate competitors. In recent years, U.S. and European global managers have grown wary of depending too heavily on Japanese

The global manager cannot bias investment decisions in favor of the corporation's home base.

companies for critical high-tech components. Specifically, they worry that Japanese suppliers will allocate the parts they make to other Japanese companies first and withhold them from foreign partners or that Japanese companies will use the parts to gain a predatory foothold, gradually displacing their foreign partner as the relationship becomes more and more lopsided.

These concerns of Western managers about Japanese corporate practice are not necessarily yielding more investment in the United States; they are leading to more alliances across the Atlantic or with non-Japanese Pacific Rim partners. For example, IBM's recent efforts to ensure itself a supply of random-access memory semiconductor chips independent of Japanese companies has led it into a spate of investments and alliances across Europe – a joint venture with Siemens, membership in the European Community's semiconductor research consortium called JESSI. IBM's strategy, like that of other Western global corporations, is not pro-United States – it is pro-IBM and non-Japanese.

In fact, as corporations spin their global webs, other corporations, rather than governments, are likely to engage in strategic countermoves. The more companies decentralize their operations, the less authority and control any single government can assert over them. A company that is comfortable investing all over the world can negotiate with governments all over the world and, with enough leverage, dictate the specific terms and conditions of its investment.

The National Interest

They, as global managers, want to increase their world market shares, profits, and share prices. *We*, as citizens of a particular nation, want to secure national wealth and national economic well-being. They parcel activities around the world according to economic criteria, putting them wherever they can get the best return, intentionally playing no favorites to avoid setting off political alarms. But we do play favorites. We feel a special allegiance to our country and to our compatriots. Global corporations exist within world markets; we are members of a society.

Our interests diverge from theirs for two specific reasons: we are concerned about our nation's relative wealth and power, and we want to capture for our nation the public benefits that spill over from global investment.

Relative Wealth and Power. Consider the following two possible scenarios for economic growth between now and the year 2000 for the United States and Japan:

The United States economy grows 20%, but the Japanese economy grows 90%.

The United States economy grows only 8%, and the Japanese economy grows 8.2%.

When I have offered this choice in classes and corporate training seminars, a majority of the Americans in my audience usually select the second option. Many Americans are more concerned with our country's relative wealth and power compared with Japan's than with our country's absolute growth. We not only want global managers to favor the United States – locating their high value-added activities in America – more than they favor Japan, but many would also sacrifice some additional wealth in order to prevent the Japanese from enjoying even greater gains. Whether or not these sentiments should be commended as a principle of international economic behavior, they cannot be ignored. Despite the logic of the global manager and the global web, national wealth and power continue to drive us to think about our national interests not only in absolute terms but also relative to our perceived national competitors.

Spillovers from Corporate Investment. Even those of us who select the first option might still want global managers to favor the United States because of national benefits that do not typically appear on the global manager's balance sheets. Specifically, these spillovers might include the jobs that result from having sophisticated factories, laboratories, and equipment in the United States, whose high wages multiply throughout the economy, raising other incomes. Good jobs also generate higher tax receipts, which permit government to invest in public facilities such as improved schools and transportation and also to care for the elderly and the disadvantaged in society. Moreover, on-the-job training and the resulting technical know-how enable Americans to innovate and thus generate more wealth for the United States in the years to come. This know-how spreads beyond individual Americans to create entire regions of U.S. innovation – the San Francisco Bay area and greater Boston in science and engineering; Los Angeles in music and film; New York in law, advertising, and publishing; Minneapolis in medical devices and instruments; Irvine and Pasadena, California in industrial design, and so on.

The logic brings us to this central issue:

Their goal is to maximize profits by siting their production activities around the world for the highest return and investing wherever it is most efficient and strategically profitable.

Our goal is to attract into the United States the most high value-added global activities with the greatest positive spillovers – and to keep and grow them here.

We can pursue our goal by ensuring that we give America's children a first-class education – starting with preschool and extending through college or vocational training – and that our transportation and communications infrastructure is second to none. But even if we make the United States an attractive place for high value-added investments, that alone will not be enough to guarantee the kind of global investment we need. In a world in which every other nation is bidding for high value-added jobs, America must negotiate as well.

The Logic of Global Negotiations

When trade was the primary engine of global economic integration and corporations were rooted in particular countries, negotiations were government-to-government. Each nation's objective was to open foreign markets to the exports of its own companies or to protect its own companies from foreign competition at home. Countries measured their success by the extent to which they were able to sell their goods and services within foreign nations and how much world market share their own companies could command.

But the new global economy renders obsolete these old forms of negotiating and keeping score. Global investment is supplanting merchandise trade as the major engine of world economic integration – and the key to a nation's wealth and well-being. And negotiations between governments and global managers – between the new "us" and the new "them" – are displacing the old government-to-government talks.

The Growing Importance of Direct Investment. Between 1983 and 1988, world trade volumes grew at a compounded annual rate of 5%. Over the same period, global direct foreign investment increased by more than 20% annually in real terms. As a result, sales by foreign-owned affiliates within a nation now typically exceed foreign exports to that nation. In fact, when the foreign sales of U.S.-owned companies are calculated against the total purchases by Americans of the products of foreign-owned companies, America's trade deficit turns into a net surplus. The foreign operations of U.S.-owned corporations now account for more than $1 trillion in annual sales around the world, roughly four times the total export of goods made in the United States and about seven to eight times the value of America's recent trade deficits.

Today much of what is actually "traded" across borders are intangible services – research, engineering, design, financial, management, marketing, and sales – transferred within global corporations from one location to another. IBM exports relatively few machines from the United States to the rest of its global web; most of its U.S. "exports" are ideas and insights. Honda now imports relatively few automotive components into the United States from Japan; most of its Japanese "imports" are technological specifications and management know-how. The threads of the new global web are computers, facsimile machines, satellites, high-resolution monitors, and modems – linking up ideas and money from each of the company's worldwide locations with every other. In 1990, some 20,000 privately leased international telephone circuits carried video images, voices, and data instantaneously back and forth among managers, engineers, and marketers working together on different continents.

The New Negotiations. This change in the locus of economic activity – from trade to direct investment – implies a change in the nature of negotiations: while we focus our attention on the Office of the United States Trade Representative in Washington, D.C., looking for government-to-government talks to open up foreign markets to the products of "our" companies, that is no longer where the important action really is. Even when these old-fashioned trade talks succeed in opening a foreign market to a U.S. company, the effect on *us*, on our incomes and standard of living, is often tangential. For example, the recent agreement secured with Japan after intense government pressure to permit Toys "R" Us to open a large retail outlet in Tokyo will have almost no effect on the U.S. work force, apart from a few U.S. managers. Almost everything that Toys "R" Us sells in Japan will be conceived, designed, and manufactured outside the United States.

Another sort of negotiation is becoming far more important – one that occurs between a different set of parties. On one side of the bargaining table still sit the government representatives; but on the other side *they* sit – the global managers. The government negotiators represent the citizens of the nation, not the nation's corporations. Their job is to induce the global managers to site certain activities in the nation and thus provide the nation's citizens with good jobs. In return, the government negotiators offer a carrot – an assortment of tax breaks, financial inducements, and public investments. There is also a stick: government negotiators may threaten to close the national market to the company unless it makes the desired investments.

Third World nations have long bargained along these lines with multinationals headquartered in advanced nations. But the logic of the global web means that practically every nation now ends up sitting on that side of the table, including some of the most unlikely parties. Hoping to attract labor-intensive light industries like electronic-parts manufacturers, Vietnam has recently created an industrial zone on the outskirts of Ho Chi Minh City; the government is prepared to negotiate rock-bottom leases to global companies willing to invest in production facilities there. In these types of negotiations, moreover, governments make virtually no distinction between domestic and foreign-owned companies. "There is no flag on capital," says Argentina's President Carlos Menem. "I ask myself, what is national capital? Is it the $50 billion in flight capital that has left the country via Argentine business executives? Or resources used by multinationals to produce here?"

America's Negotiators. Like every other nation, the United States is taking an active part in these new sorts of negotiations. But unlike other countries, we are not represented by a high-ranking federal official like the United States Trade Representative. Instead, we are represented by 50 state governors and hundreds of mayors and city man-

> In the bidding for global investment, U.S. bargaining agents often compete against themselves.

agers. Like the bargaining agents of other nations, these governors and mayors pay no attention to the nationality of the global managers on the other side of the table. In fact, 43 U.S. states maintain permanent offices and staffs in foreign capitals to conduct negotiations with foreign managers full-time. And these offices are not limited to the major commercial centers of the world: 10 states have recently opened offices in Taipei, and 4 more have announced plans to locate there. Just as often, the global managers sitting across the table are American, whose companies are headquartered in the United States – but they drive just as hard a bargain as the global managers from other countries.

The process works in a crude but effective fashion: the possibility of a new factory, laboratory, headquarters, or branch office within a state or a city sets off a furious auction; a casual threat to move an ex-

isting facility starts an equally impassioned round of negotiation. The governor or mayor who successfully lures or keeps the jobs is a hero; the one who loses the bidding may soon lose his or her own job.

The problem for us is that our U.S. bargaining agents often compete against themselves. A case in point: in the early 1980s, the Hyster Corporation, a manufacturer of forklift trucks, notified public officials in eight locations where Hyster had factories – five U.S. states, three foreign locations – that some of the facilities would be closed. Hyster invited each political jurisdiction to bid to keep its local jobs. The resulting auction was a great success for Hyster. By the time the bidding had closed, American states and cities had surrendered a total of $18 million to preserve about 2,000 Hyster jobs. The big "winner" was Danville, Illinois – a town with a population of only 39,000. In exchange for 850 blue-collar jobs, Danville and the state of Illinois agreed to provide Hyster with roughly $10,000 in subsidies.

Just as frequently, these kinds of auctions are global affairs. For example, when Diamond Star Motors, the Mitsubishi-Chrysler joint venture, announced in 1985 that it would begin assembling automobiles in the United States, four states competed for the factory. Illinois came out the winner with a bid of ten years of direct aid and incentives worth $276 million – roughly $25,000 for every new job the factory would create in the state. The city of Bloomington, Illinois threw in an additional $10 million of land and $20 million in local tax abatements.

Over time, the bidding has become more ferocious and the incentives more generous. In 1980, Tennessee paid the equivalent of $11,000 per job to entice Nissan to Smyrna. By 1986, Indiana had to spend $50,000 per job to induce Subaru-Isuzu to set up shop in Lafayette. When ConAgra threatened to leave Omaha, the state of Nebraska felt the heat of the bidding war directly. "It's like a poker game," said Donald Pursell, former director of Nebraska's Bureau of Business Research. "Nebraska makes a bid, Iowa ups it."

Bidding to attract new plants or keep existing ones requires that such state and local largess be routinely parceled out. Few global managers expect to pay the same rate of property tax in proportion to the assessed value of their land as local residents pay. Using the threat of the global web, it is relatively easy for global mangers to insist on a better deal simply by pointing out to state or local officials that, without more favorable tax treatment, the company will move to one of its other global locations. Partly as a result of this kind of leverage, corporations now contribute a much smaller percentage of local taxes in the United States than they did in the past. In

1957, corporations accounted for about 45% of local revenues; by 1989, corporate taxes comprised only 16%.

Paradoxically, such tax breaks and subsidies make it more difficult for states and communities to finance public education and infrastructure. For example, General Motors's successful effort to cut its annual taxes by $1 million in Tarrytown, New York, where the company has had a factory since 1914, has forced the town to lay off dozens of teachers and administrators and to cut back on school supplies and routine school maintenance. Ultimately, these kinds of "beggar thy neighbor" ploys by some global managers undermine our ability to attract global investments – since the quality of the work force, good transportation facilities, and a good quality of life are ultimately more important lures for attracting global managers' investments than tax concessions and subsidies.

The Advantages of Bargaining as a Whole. It is simple common sense that large nations that bargain as a whole with global managers – or groups of smaller nations that pool their bargaining strength behind a single agent – have much more clout than small nations or separate states and cities. By avoiding internal bidding contests, they end up paying far less to attract investment and have an easier time getting the jobs they want when and where they want them. For example, the European Commission reviews location incentives offered by member nations in order to minimize bidding by one against the other. As a result, when Honda decided in 1989 to locate its first European plant in Britain, it did not receive a shilling of inducement from Downing Street.

After 1992, a united Europe will be in an even stronger bargaining position in negotiations with global managers. Access to Europe's newly integrated market of 230 million people will itself be a powerful lure. Global managers are already scrambling to set up facilities there in anticipation that Europe's gates will shut. "You can't pick up a piece of paper that says why Intel has got to manufac-

> No one would seriously propose that each U.S. state conduct its own foreign trade policy.

ture in Europe," one Intel executive told a reporter. "The rules don't exist." But when they do, Intel wants to be already well-established inside the gates.

Another illustration of the same principle: for years, before Japan caught up with the West technologically, Japan's Ministry of International Trade and Industry acted as a single bargaining agent for the country, acquiring foreign technology at cut-rate prices. By effectively barring auctions for licenses in Japan, MITI forced foreign licensors to sell at a fraction of the cost of developing the technology originally. According to estimates, between 1956 and 1978 Japan paid some $9 billion to acquire U.S. technologies that cost between $500 billion and $1 trillion to develop.

The Logic of a *United* States of America

Think back to any earlier time. Before the ratification of the U.S. Constitution, every state carried out its own trade policy, negotiating separate trade pacts with foreign nations. This approach allowed the other nations – Britain in particular – to play one state against another, gaining agreements that favored Britain at the expense of the states.

When John Adams, representing the Continental Congress, sought Britain's agreement to open its ports to U.S. shippers, British Foreign Secretary Charles James Fox contemptuously suggested that ambassadors from all 13 states would have to sign any such treaty. As a result, when the founding fathers met in Philadelphia to devise a new constitution, they agreed with little debate that Congress should have the power to "regulate commerce with foreign nations and among the several states." This unprepossessing clause in Article I became the charter of our national economy.

Today no one would seriously propose that each U.S. state conduct its own foreign trade policy. That responsibility is firmly lodged in the federal government. Trade negotiations are centralized in the Office of the United States Trade Representative, with its own expert staff. But today, with direct investment supplanting trade as the engine of world commerce, we lack any similar vehicle to negotiate on our behalf with global managers. As a consequence, we are relatively easy pickings for them.

What is needed is a shift of authority over global investment, from states and cities to the federal government. What little authority the federal government now exercises over global investment is negative. That is, under the Omnibus Trade Act of 1988, the federal government can block foreign investors from gaining a controlling interest in a U.S.-owned corporation if the purchase is likely to "impair national security." Under several other recent statutes, the federal government subsidizes private sector R&D only if it is undertaken by a U.S.-owned company. Even more recently, Congress has sought to impose special tax and disclosure burdens on non-U.S. companies operating in the United States.

Most of these investment disincentives make little sense. Global managers at U.S.-owned companies are no more "us" than are the global managers of non-U.S. companies. And it is in our interests to attract investment from global managers all over the world, rather than raising investment barriers on the faulty basis of national identity. Most important, while other nations are improving their bargaining power to attract global investment, the United States continues both to dissipate its bargaining power by permitting state and local bidding wars and to discourage foreign investment by creating federal barriers.

A United States Investment Representative. A response that would serve our interests and accede to the logic of the global manager and the global web is both the creation of an Office of the United States Investment Representative, paralleling the United States Trade Representative, and the preemption by federal law of separate state and local laws that authorize their officials to offer investment incentives. In other words, the federal government should effectively bar states and cities from bidding for global capital; just as the USTR negotiates national trade issues, the USIR would negotiate investment issues.

The USIR would determine what sorts of global investments we need in order to enhance our wealth

> Other nations are improving their bargaining power to attract global investment; America still creates federal barriers.

and create important spillovers, but which would not be made without special incentives. Do we want more of the public benefits associated with microelectronic fabrication and manufacturing? More microbiological research? More state-of-the-art auto assembly plants? Just as important, where do we want to see these investments located – in regions of high unemployment and relatively low skills? In regions where there already exist the beginnings of a critical mass of suppliers and relevant skills? The USIR would also monitor major factories, laboratories,

and offices in the United States that global managers were planning to close and move abroad. Is it worth trying to keep them here? Why, and at what cost?

The tools available to the USIR in negotiating on our behalf already exist but are now scattered across the national landscape: tax abatements, tax credits, R&D incentives, loans and loan guarantees, use of public lands, public capital investment, and more. Moreover, working with the USTR, the USIR could offer trade concessions in exchange for the investments we seek – lowering tariffs on certain components to be used in the proposed U.S. manufacturing facility, providing relief from voluntary restraint agreements on other parts and components, granting immunity from certain antidumping levies. And if other nations threaten to close off their markets to global corporations unless they make certain investments there, America would be in the position to use similar threats as a means of ensuring its fair share of such investments.

The creation of a USIR would thus solve four problems at the same time. By pooling our now diffuse bargaining power, the USIR could bargain more effectively and at a lower cost on our behalf – thus preserving scarce resources for the important tasks of educating our work force and building a world-class infrastructure. It would bargain only for those global investments that promised large beneficial spillovers and that would not come to our shores automatically. It would seek to guide these investments to locations that would maximize the benefit to us. And it would put America on an equal footing with other large nations and emerging trading blocs that are already bidding effectively for global investment.

Without question, the activities of the USIR would be the subject of intense political interest. State and local governments would still compete against each other, but the competition would be contained among us, rather than channeled as payments to global corporations. And yes, the USIR would be selecting certain technologies and industries as more critical than others – which is exactly what Carla Hills, the United States Trade Representative, does now when she gives priority to certain industries during trade negotiations.

A GATT for Direct Investment. Just as we need a United States Investment Representative to parallel the efforts of the United States Trade Representative, so we need a GATT for Direct Investment to parallel the GATT that establishes rules for global trade – and for precisely the same reasons. So long as relative economic wealth and power figure prominently in national calculations, some framework for negotiations is necessary – lest nations fall prey to the same zero-sum investment bidding as America's states now engage in. Moreover, in the absence of such a new international forum, wealthy nations will always have the capacity to outbid poorer ones.

A GATT for Direct Investment would establish international rules by which nations bid for global investment and processes for settling disputes over such bids. For example, threats to close off a domestic market unless certain investments were made in it would be carefully circumscribed – for it is precisely threats such as these that rapidly unravel into zero-sum contests. The amount of permissible subsidies to attract investment might be proportional to the size of the nation's work force, but inversely proportional to its average skills – so that nations with large and relatively unskilled work forces would be allowed greater leeway in bidding for global investments than nations with smaller and more highly skilled work forces.

Other kinds of investment subsidies would be pooled and parceled out to where they could do the most good globally, as the European Community has begun to do regionally. For instance, nations would agree to fund jointly those basic research projects whose fruits are likely to travel across international borders almost immediately – projects such as the high-energy particle accelerator and the exploration of space. How such funds were apportioned and toward what ends would, of course, be subject to negotiation. The rules of the GATT for Direct Investment would also specify fair allocations of tax payments by companies operating across several borders and would reconcile various regulatory regimes.

Come back to the global negotiating table where we started. We are on one side; they are on the other.

There is nothing sinister or hostile about this setting. It is, in fact, an inevitable, practically inexorable extension of the emerging global economy. It is not, however, absolutely true that our interests

---

Global managers are adapting with agility; U.S. government lags behind momentous events unfolding around the globe.

---

and theirs conflict. Both sides, for example, benefit from our having a well-educated, well-trained work force; a well-developed, well-maintained public infrastructure; a high-quality environment and a high overall standard of living.

But there are differences as well, places where our interests naturally diverge. Many global managers, more sensitive to the requirements of the bottom line and thus more agile in adapting, have realized the implications of globalization. We and our governments are still struggling to catch up. They are changing the shape, size, location, and operating principles of global businesses. We are mired in the obsolete practices and attitudes of a previous era; our government lags behind the epoch-shaping events unfolding around the globe. Other nations – other groups of "us" – are reacting to these same events: EC '92, Japan's cautious emergence in world councils. Now we must move in the United States to create the new institutions and new attitudes that will permit us to negotiate effectively with them – that will allow us to negotiate as if our future depended on it. ▽

Reprint 91206

1992 promises crucial negotiations for American business. The U.S. government is torn by conflicting national values.

Can the U.S. Negotiate for Trade Equality?

by Raymond Vernon

For U.S. managers preoccupied with international competition, the course just ahead is uncharted. In almost any market in which Americans hope to sell their goods and services or expand their enterprises, there are as many opportunities as threats – and plenty of both in Europe as it approaches 1992.

One thing is reasonably sure: the actions of the U.S. government, especially in the fields of trade policy and monetary policy, are likely to be critical in determining how American business will fare. At the same time, the economies of the leading countries are now deeply intertwined. National political leaders are increasingly forced to choose between international cooperation or losses that damage us all.

Their collective efforts to deal with common economic problems are making headway. But the U.S. government, more than any other taking part in these international exchanges, is torn by conflicting national values. Americans place a high value on the diffusion of bureaucratic power and on the participa-

Raymond Vernon is Herbert F. Johnson Professor Emeritus of International Business Management and Clarence Dillon Professor Emeritus of International Affairs at Harvard University. He is the author (with Debora L. Spar) of the recently published Beyond Globalism: Remaking American Foreign Economic Policy *(Free Press, 1989).*

tion of the public in policy-making. At the same time, they prefer an international economic environment that is open – and stable. American negotiators, in consequence, are supported by a fragmented decision-making structure that was never designed to shape and implement foreign economic policies.

Falling Barriers in Europe's Market

What uncertainties exist in the European market? Only three or four years ago, Europe's business community seemed half-paralyzed by pessimism and drift, squeezed between Japanese and U.S. juggernauts. Domestic markets were shrinking, and products aimed at global markets were failing. As is well known, the 12 members of the European Community (EC) responded by setting the ambitious goal of completing a European common market by 1992, an enlarged internal market for Europe that would be as open as that of the United States. (Presumably, the customs officials posted at Europe's internal borders would lose their functions, because services and capital as well as goods and people would flow without restraint.)

This decision for economic union has transformed the mood of European economic and corporate leaders and created a wave of initiatives reminiscent of the 1960s. Granted, the problems of economic union are staggering, with differences in national tax regimes topping the list. Yet 40 years ago, the EC's founders astutely foresaw that the member countries could be dragged into a common market by *engrenage*—literally, the process of being caught up in the teeth of a grinder. Today their prophecy seems

> ## The U.S. decision-making structure was never designed to shape trade policy.

on the way to being realized. EC members are being pulled almost inexorably toward closer association. Outside of Europe, the full implications of this change have yet to sink in.

Among the restraints the member countries hope to eliminate are so-called technical provisions. These include national standards applied ostensibly for safety or health reasons that also serve to hold down foreign competition, such as standards for electric heaters and bicycle brakes. The European Commission has been nibbling away at such measures. Negotiations for more open markets promise to accelerate sharply. Slated for removal are restrictions on the sale of financial services such as insurance and banking. And EC officials hope to cut down on the "buy at home" practices of governments, state-owned enterprises, and regulated monopolies like electric utilities and telephone companies.

To be sure, Europe's new economic policies will mean business for companies operating both inside and outside of Europe by enlarging the size of the internal market and by eliminating barriers that favor national producers. But at the same time, these policies can create new hardships for certain outsiders, especially those already selling to Europe, by diverting trade with non-European companies to new competitors emerging from inside the club. In the 1960s, in the decade following its creation, the EC reduced restrictions on trade in manufactured goods not only with its members but also with outside companies. That felicitous step, achieved through a GATT-sponsored round of negotiations—the so-called Kennedy Round—generated many new opportunities for foreign companies, especially American ones. At the same time, however, the EC developed a preferential system that hobbled foreign agricultural suppliers.

Coinciding with the European unification effort is a formidable round of GATT trade negotiations.

Launched by the 96 members of GATT in 1986, these negotiations will likely continue through the next four years and will take the industrialized countries into new territory. For the past 40 years, GATT members have concentrated mainly on reducing tariffs and other restrictions on the international movement of merchandise. But in 1986, at the urging of the United States, the member countries agreed to take up existing restrictions on international trade in services, on patent and trademark rights, and on investment regulations, especially those that affect international trade. The GATT negotiations could cover a vast array of trade issues, from banking to ocean transport and from engineering to insurance.

It is worth emphasizing that U.S. export of services promises to compose a growing part of U.S. exports as a whole. Designing, installing, and operating information systems, for instance, may together prove as big an export in the future as machine tools have been in the past. And the ability of the U.S. economy to export its services is closely linked—indeed, increasingly linked—to its ability to export products and to manage foreign direct investments. The sale of such products typically demands demonstration, training, and installation, as well as adaptation, maintenance, and repair. Especially in high-tech fields, the sale of products has become inseparable from the provision of services and the establishment of affiliates in foreign countries.

The Executive: Playing under Handicaps?

As the European union and the GATT negotiations progress concurrently (both are expected to wind up by June 1993), there is sure to be considerable overlap in subject matter—especially with respect to the international sale of services. The odds are high that the two negotiations will become intertwined and that vital U.S. interests will ride on the outcome. Is the U.S. government inherently limited in its ability to cope with these negotiations? Is it restricted by its own precedents and politics?

In the past, whenever U.S. trade representatives have faced off against those of other governments, they have had the substantial advantage of representing a country with the greatest economic, political, and military resources. At the same time, they have labored under the handicap of mutually inconsistent goals and diffuse negotiating authority. Americans no longer have the advantage. What of the handicaps?

Consider the matter of "free trade." In spite of quadrennial outbursts of campaign hyperbole, both

Democratic and Republican administrations have stood for free trade—the proposition that open, competitive markets are better than closed markets. This consensus explains why the president's powers to negotiate for the reduction of tariffs and other trade barriers have been routinely renewed since 1945 in a series of trade acts, legislation typically supported by lawmakers from both parties. It explains why, in 1979, in conjunction with the "Tokyo Round," Congress adopted innovative codes leading to freer trade by a vote that was almost unanimous. It ex-

> ## U.S. negotiators may want free trade, but domestic interest groups can always challenge their agreements.

plains why Congress overwhelmingly ratified free trade with Canada in 1988. Even the Trade Act of 1988, which mandated the president to retaliate against countries that effectively close their markets to U.S. business, was as much a statement in favor of the free flow of goods and services as a warning that the U.S. government would protect key American producers.

If free trade were the *only* value that Americans all seemed to agree on, U.S. trade representatives would not be especially handicapped. In most such negotiations, however, U.S. representatives must be responsive to another widely shared value, one that sharply distinguishes the preferences of Americans from those of most other countries. This is the deep-seated desire of Americans to limit the power of the executive by the hallowed system of checks and balances.

Several laws passed in the last few decades have strengthened the checks and balances under which the executive must operate. In no other country do we find the equivalent of U.S. freedom-of-information laws, congressional vetoes of executive action, and powers by which the courts can restrict other government branches. Legislation under the generic heading of "government in the sunshine" has contributed to a general ethos in which there is a widespread presumption that those outside the government have a right to know what is going on inside the government. Indeed, the increasing complexity of U.S. trade legislation is largely the result of Congress's efforts to strengthen the citizen's or corporation's rights of challenge.

This poses a basic dilemma. When the executive negotiates on any issue with other countries—whether to lower a tariff or to license a bank—it is with the understanding that U.S. action will be con-

strained along with the actions of our trading partners. But our partners will hardly take seriously the positions presented by U.S. representatives if the latter are routinely subject to the challenges of domestic interest groups.

The American public's aversion to creating a strong executive can be seen also in the diffuse structure of the executive branch itself. Anyone who has leafed through the pages of the *Congressional Directory* is struck by the great proliferation of "independent agencies" that are clustered within the branch. Agencies such as the Securities and Exchange Commission, the Consumer Product Safety Commission, and the Environmental Protection Agency can act with considerable independence. In most cases, they possess quasi-legislative powers to adopt rules and quasi-judicial powers to decide cases independently of the White House. Getting these agencies to move in tandem in an international negotiation promises to present a staggering challenge to the American system of government.

The leadership of such agencies, incidentally, is usually transient, drawn from among the 4,000 political appointees who change with each administration. Some of these appointees are as knowledgeable and energetic in their fields as the permanent, career civil servants whom they are appointed to manage. Most, however, are tyros who need substantial exposure before they can make use of the empty desks and file cabinets they encounter when they take office. Moreover, most of them have no intention of shaping government policy over the long pull; they will typically hold their jobs for only a few years before returning to the private sector. Continuity and consistency will be hard to achieve.

Congressional Power

And then there is the Congress. The Constitution squarely puts responsibility for international trade on its shoulders. Article 1, Section 8 directs it "to regulate Commerce with foreign Nations." And the president's powers in trade policy are dependent on explicit delegations by Congress.

To be sure, ever since Congress passed the Trade Agreement Act of 1934, it has recognized that such delegations of power are necessary if the president is to be in a position to cooperate with other governments. Nevertheless, Congress has always been careful to protect its own constitutional rights, especially when the interests of constituents are involved. Accordingly, every bill renewing the president's authority to negotiate on trade matters has carried one or more new provisions expanding Americans' rights to institute special actions for redress.

With the Trade Act of 1988, the schizophrenia of the Congress—promote open markets, protect constituent interests—has produced disconcerting results. Nearly 1,200 pages in length, the trade act was the product of over 40 subcommittees. The conference committee appointed to reconcile differences between House and Senate versions of the bill included nearly 40% of the congressional membership. In a few spare words, the new law authorizes the president to engage in the negotiations contemplated under GATT. But in many thousands of added words, it seeks to circumscribe that power and to facilitate challenges to future trade measures.

At present, prospects seem good that challenges will come in a steady stream. In the past, there were struggles over chicken, pasta flour, steel, and semiconductors. These will multiply in number. Although the U.S. national interest requires a clear eye on the wider issues in Europe and in GATT, the president may not be able to turn his attention from these narrower cases for very long.

The U.S. position will be hampered also by the fact that it has always waffled between two sharply differ-

> ## Congress can't make up its mind about "national treatment."

ent principles, that of "reciprocity" and that of "national treatment." For example, the official U.S. position is that U.S. enterprises setting up subsidiaries in foreign countries should be entitled to "national treatment," that is, the same treatment under the laws of foreign countries that the nationals of those countries receive. On the other hand, the United States rejects national treatment as the criterion for dealing with patent rights. (If a foreign country decides that no inventor, whether national or foreign, is entitled to receive a patent on a pharmaceutical invention, the country is liable to punishment under new U.S. trade law even though it is providing national treatment.)

U.S. policymakers are no more loyal to the "reciprocity" rule. Congress has embraced reciprocity for sanctioning the establishment of foreign-owned telecommunications companies in the United States by specifying that countries failing to match the open nature of the U.S. telecommunications market risk losing access to it. Yet U.S. policymakers hesitate to invoke reciprocity when considering what rights they should demand for U.S. banks operating abroad.

U.S. banking restrictions, imposed by state laws, Treasury regulations, and the Glass-Steagall Act, are so pervasive that foreign banks operating in the United States often have far less freedom than they would have operating at home. (These confusions are not made any easier by the vague and obfuscatory phrases—like "level playing field" and "unfair trade practices"—that come so naturally to congressional debaters.)

Eventually, governments may well come to some consensus regarding those areas to be administered according to reciprocity and those according to national treatment. But before progress can be made on that front, U.S. policymakers must stop drawing ideas as if from a smorgasbord.

Europe's Difficulties—and Ours

Even if the U.S. government manages to overcome the structural obstacles impeding its own capacity to prepare for the negotiations with the Community and with GATT, the European countries present obstacles in their own right. France, Britain, and Italy have barely reconciled themselves to surrendering their powers over tariffs, subsidies, and other regulations. With the 1992 decision, the EC's reach extends much more deeply into each national economy.

Accordingly, issues formerly perceived as primarily of national concern and responsibility will now become Community matters, subject to legislation and litigation in Community institutions. Areas likely to fall under EC jurisdiction include consumer and bank depositor safety, attorney and accountant qualifications, corporate disclosure practices, control of the environment, and governmental procurement practices.

The transition will not be easy. Member governments are bound to have second thoughts. And where the jurisdiction of the Community appears less than wholly secure, member governments are likely to take national measures to challenge it. While beating out internal differences in the Community, European governments will have little stomach for weighing the complaints of outsiders. Yet such complaints cannot be avoided: any measure that improves members' access to one another's territories risks doing so at the expense of third countries, especially in the short run.

As in the 1960s, numerous U.S. industries will again see *their* interests at stake as Europe labors toward the difficult 1992 goals. U.S. exporters who wish to sell their products in Italian markets against French or German competition, for instance, will discover that Italy, though bound to accept the adequacy of the health and safety standards of its fellow Europeans, has no obligation to accept U.S. standards as adequate. U.S. bankers who want to sell their services in the Italian markets will worry, understandably, that their European rivals may acquire an inside track.

An important principle by which the Community intends to improve mutual access will only accentuate the disparities between the rights of members and the rights of nonmembers like the United States. The European Commission sets standards for, say, environmental or consumer protection. When a member regulates domestic production of specific goods or services to meet these standards, its measures and prescriptions are presumed to satisfy the regulatory requirements of *all other members*. Accordingly, the measures that Italy prescribes for making toys safe for children will have to be accepted as adequate in France—so long as Italy's measures conform to the EC's general directives. Will this leave the United States out of the loop?

The obvious solution is for the EC as a whole to exchange similar rights with nonmembers. But is this realistic? Within the Community, members' rights can be administered, adjudicated, and extended by common institutions, including the European Commission, Council of Ministers, Court of Justice, and Parliament. The members share goals and have the means to adjudicate disputes over the meaning of agreements. No corresponding institutions exist to handle disputes between the Community and nonmember countries.

The dispute procedures of GATT, it is true, have had a remarkable record, especially considering the feebleness of the authority on which they are based and the indifference with which Congress has received their findings. But GATT procedures are not by themselves the institutions that will be needed to reduce or eliminate the frictions that are bound to emerge between Europe and the rest of the world.

International Cooperation: Pessimists and Optimists

The argument to this point raises the question whether tensions created by the EC's 1992 program bode well or ill for future international economic cooperation. The pessimist will expect discord between the Community and other countries. The optimist will see new opportunities for governments to establish more effective institutions to deal with chronic problems in their economic relations.

The prospects for the GATT negotiations, alas, offer thinner grounds for optimism. The pessimists have the stronger case, in light of both the heterogeneity of GATT interests, values, and institutions and the precedents set by 40 years of negotiations under GATT's auspices.

It is by now a deeply rooted tenet in GATT negotiations that developing countries fall into a special class, entitled to the benefits of liberalizing measures of advanced countries but not obliged to reciprocate with measures of their own. Two generations of eco-

> It is time to empower international institutions to settle trade disputes—like the U.S. and Canada have done.

nomic diplomats, led by Brazil and India and supported discretely by other beneficiaries such as Korea, have staunchly defended their position.

The United States, for its part, has tried for more than a decade to persuade some developing countries—those that have proven their ability to industrialize and export successfully—gradually to assume the GATT obligations already borne by more industrialized members. But to little avail. A few countries, such as Singapore, have shown a willingness to modify their exemptions. Most have found it hard to curb the exercise of a right so long and successfully exploited.

Besides, the GATT negotiations are to cover areas of trade in which most developing countries feel themselves at an overwhelming disadvantage. Korea, Brazil, Taiwan, and some other industrializing countries may feel competent in steel, textiles, and other manufactures, but they see themselves hopelessly behind in insurance, banking, accounting, air travel, and other services. And most developing countries see their defense of the right to retain freedom of action in such areas as patent law and investment restrictions as a most important negotiating objective. Chances are slim that these countries will be willing to join in agreements that the United States, Europe, and Japan find acceptable among themselves.

What, then, is it reasonable to press for? Some of the most striking recent examples of international cooperation have resulted from business communities concluding that agreement was preferable to continued anarchy. Consider the extensive network of bilateral treaties between advanced countries that deal with taxation of foreign income. Multinational enterprises all over the world gave their support to treaty negotiations, preferring agreement to the risk of having each government tax their foreign income without regard for taxes paid to other governments. Since 1975, there has also been an extraordinary string of agreements between bank supervisory authorities. These agreements have strengthened the creditworthiness of banks engaged in international business and would have been altogether unlikely had the banks themselves not supported them.

Perhaps the most fundamental step the United States could take is one found in the extraordinary provisions of the new U.S.-Canada free-trade agreement—provisions strongly supported by business communities on both sides of the border. That agreement breaks new ground in establishing elaborate channels for settling disputes between the two governments. One especially interesting provision allows each party to protest an action by the other through an appeals procedure governed by an international tribunal; a tribunal composed of two judges from Canada and the United States each, with a fifth judge chosen by them. The willingness of the United States to agree to such an international body in which Americans will pursue their challenges creates a precedent of extraordinary significance.

This is a time of vast change in the international environment and of unprecedented response to such change. But old national values, cherished and protected over long periods of time, are not to be abandoned in the wink of an eye. The challenge for U.S. business and government is to find new responses that serve both our tested values and the drastically changed international environment in which they must be put to work.

Reprint 89313

"A good example of what you can accomplish when you don't have to contend with unions and inflationary material costs."

The China trade: making the deal

Lucian W. Pye

In the first nine months of 1985, U.S. companies formed more than 800 joint ventures with state enterprises in the People's Republic of China—compared with only about 900 in the previous five years. Despite this seeming explosion, real—financial—commitment has not yet occurred. Direct American investment totals only about $1 billion out of $14.6 billion of all foreign investment in China; if you exclude offshore oil exploration, the figure dwindles to about $150 million.

> *"Many U.S. CEOs have been caught up in the 'Westchester County syndrome.' They rush over to China simply to score points at the country club."*

U.S. executives often fail to reach real commitments because they can't get the knack of Chinese negotiating practices. The Chinese may be less developed in technology and industrial organization than we, but for centuries they have known few peers in the subtle art of negotiating.

When measured against the effort and skill the Chinese bring to the bargaining table, American executives fall short. They often seem unsure about priorities and vacillate about their purposes. When compounded by the headlong enthusiasm Americans show at the general prospect of any new market—and China's market is a vision of one billion people—such uncertainty is a serious liability.

Part of the reason priorities remain uncertain is that executives feign initial interest as a public relations ploy to prove to stockholders how up with the times they are. CEOs get caught up in what has been called the "Westchester County syndrome"; they believe they can score points at their country clubs or

among business associates by boasting that they've just been to China. When post-Maoist China opened up to U.S. business, a flock of such executives rushed over and rather casually and enthusiastically negotiated letters of intent. Then they sent subordinates abroad who had to work out the contractual details. Because they had made commitments, however vague and undefined they seemed at the time, the first visitors had played into Chinese hands. Further negotiations turned the generalities into formal agreements. These pacts gave the Chinese undue and definite advantages.

Chinese negotiators respond to our seeming lack of thought with tactics that are almost certain to make us feel that we have been taken. While U.S. executives nurture unreasoned hopes about capturing the China market, the Chinese come back with a very clear priority about the acquisition of advanced technologies or assistance in selling abroad to earn foreign exchange. Then when Americans finally get down to negotiating a particular contract, the Chinese return to generalities before they will discuss specifics. The result is often confusion and no deal.

Broadening commercial relations will unquestionably benefit the interests of both countries. But all sorts of negotiating roadblocks have worked against successful agreements. Some are these differences in priorities; others are cultural in orientation. Although I cannot give detailed suggestions for handling a particular deal, I want to sensitize U.S. businesspeople—to the rationale of Chinese practice. Executives who learn the rules will find that they can have fruitful associations with Chinese trading partners.

Mr. Pye, Ford Professor of Political Science at MIT, is a specialist on Asian affairs. He has been an adviser to U.S. government officials negotiating with the Chinese, and his research on the experiences of American and Japanese business negotiators led to his book, Chinese Commercial Negotiating Styles *(Oelgeschlager, Gunn and Hain, Inc.). His most recent book is* Asian Power and Politics *(Harvard University Press).*

Chinese rules

American difficulties surface from the very beginning. Companies often, for example, find it hard to choose among possible partners—especially because they can't pin down their particular capabilities. Some Chinese enterprises have limited geographical scope. Others, compartmentalized along functional lines, are severely constrained by the government's bureaucracy. Consequently, few potential associates can promise exclusive rights to the Chinese market. In 1985, a large Midwestern cable manufacturer thought its contract with a Chinese state enterprise had guaranteed exclusive rights, then discovered a French competitor had made a better deal with another company.

More important, once Americans make this agonizing choice, they find they've only cleared a preliminary hurdle. The Chinese seem to step back from an actual agreement and begin negotiations by presenting a letter of understanding that outlines general principles. U.S. managers are often put off because they want to reduce misunderstandings by immediately getting to details. They're not averse to the rhetoric of preambles, but they want to build a relationship on facts that can't be argued with. For their part, the Chinese stress friendly introductions as a way of establishing the relationship's dynamics and determining its character. Their rationale is pragmatic: in laying down general guidelines for all future dealings, they gain leverage that they can use later by calling the partner to task for not abiding by the principles. Americans think this process is only a warm-up ritual. They believe that once hard bargaining begins, positive personal feelings should not intrude except to reinforce a basic level of trust.

As I have said, Americans do sign such letters of understanding, but usually because they don't understand what can happen next. For example, Westinghouse Canada thought that it was well on its way to selling some large steam turbines to the Dong Fang Steam Turbine Works of Chungdu when the company worked out a letter of understanding with a Chinese team visiting North America. What followed, however, was not a sale but two sessions of intense negotiations in Beijing. The Canadians made all the first moves and were then counterpunched by the Chinese, who pressured Westinghouse to live up to the spirit of the original understanding by accepting a lower price. Only after the Canadian team had returned home for a second time was an agreement reached, by telex.

The story of the reopening of diplomatic relations between the United States and China in 1972 also illustrates the point. Henry Kissinger abandoned the long-standing American focus on specific issues and entered into negotiations with Zhou Enlai and Mao Zedong by concentrating on a general agreement to cooperate.

Kissinger played down particular problems because he wanted to stress the symbolic importance of a new relationship, create the general impression of great developments, and unnerve Moscow by suggesting that the balance of power in the world might change. He easily went along with the Chinese preference for communiqués and statements that defined general principles. In turn, however, the Chinese would repeatedly pressure him by declaring that Washington did not live up to the spirit of the principles.

In contrast, Secretary of State Cyrus Vance negotiated from the typical American lawyer's need to clarify certain issues and win agreement on details. Of course, Vance was forced to get more specific because he had to work out precisely the way relations would be normalized and formal diplomatic ties established. The Chinese clearly preferred Kissinger, whom they believed they could manipulate because of his sensitivity to the relationship's symbolic dimensions. In retrospect, Kissinger probably tried to sweep too much under the carpet and left his successors too many difficult problems. He probably also erred in creating an atmosphere that gave the Chinese license to warn Washington it would damage the entire relationship if it did not yield to Chinese wishes on the tough, concrete issues.

Establishing the relationship

Even with such caveats, however, those U.S. executives who build up their relationships with the Chinese by making certain that the spirit and not just the letter of a contract is followed will succeed.

Otis Elevator Company, which had a prewar operation in China, searched for a solid relationship after China's reopening that would endure through the ups and downs of a transitional period. Otis's contract with a company in Tianjin is like a marriage arrangement. For better or worse, the two partners have agreed to work things out over 30 years. In this spirit, Otis has not even pressed for a firm commitment to an exact schedule for the repatriation of profits.

In contrast, Nike has taken on and abandoned a series of partners in a frustrating search for a Chinese business that can produce shoes more cheaply than the company's Korean and Taiwanese associates— but that still meet Nike's quality standards.

Remember that the Chinese will reaffirm a relationship with a Western partner time and time again. The depth of what is possible is often incomprehensible to U.S. executives. The manager of a California company, for example, spent nearly two months in central China working out a joint venture with a provincial enterprise. The day after the agreement was signed, the other members of the team left for home and the executive remained. He met one last time with his Chinese counterpart who astounded him by raising again the issues that had been big stumbling blocks during negotiations. Even though he felt isolated, the manager defended the agreement passionately. Only much later did he understand that the contract is not as important as the potential long-range relationship. The Chinese reopened the discussion after contract signing because they considered the two parties now old friends who could bring matters up anytime.

At the heart of Chinese bargaining, a predictable psychological dimension takes the form of getting the other party to exaggerate its capabilities while the Chinese reserve the right to ask for more. Flattery is too crude a description for this process. Instead, the Chinese use the advantage a weaker party has in extracting favors from the strong—all the while maintaining its dignity. The Chinese approach calls for elaborate courtesy, gestured humility, and high sensitivity to perceived insult.

The U.S. executive's desire to enter into negotiations with outgoing, upbeat enthusiasm plays right into the strengths of this style. The Chinese believe that Americans are easily flattered, hence readily manipulated. The result is a narrow range in which the foreign negotiator can maneuver.

The Chinese approach works well with people who can easily be made to feel they are doing the wrong thing. Chinese negotiators will, for example, test U.S. executives by bringing up past mistreatment of China in the hope they will be more obliging. An executive of a large American bank now admits he got off on the wrong foot with the Chinese because he believed he could gain their confidence by vigorously criticizing past U.S. policies toward China. From then on, the Chinese did not allow him to forget that the United States had been in the wrong.

Another psychological advantage the Chinese enjoy comes from the advantage of playing the hosts. Because a visit to China gives them prestige, U.S. businesspeople accept hospitality from the Chinese even though their home-court advantage has proved significant. As guests, the Americans must adjust to Chinese norms and practices and not be rude by insisting on their own. American negotiators are usually confronted with a Chinese team that is larger—often including specialists who are interested only in solving their own engineering problems.

The owner of a New Jersey carpet company that bought the entire production of several Chinese factories became such an indebted guest that he

"Sure it's a partnership, Elwood, but it's a limited partnership, and you're the one who's limited."

began to pay nearly twice what he should have for his semiannual purchases. He would never have allowed such a thing to happen in India or Iran, but he justifies the higher prices he must charge for these products on the grounds that a market infatuated with anything Chinese will pay for such extravagances. Most important, he hopes the Chinese will reciprocate with lower prices eventually.

As hosts, the Chinese take advantage of their control over the pace of negotiations. First they set the agenda, then they suggest that the Americans start the discussions. This forces the guests to show their hand—their proposals become the starting point from which all compromises follow. To keep the process going, the Chinese expect the visitor to make the next concession, which the Chinese easily counter by asking for further concessions.

Sino-American diplomatic negotiations have followed this pattern since 1972. Either the secretary of state or the president would travel to China to gain public relations triumphs, and they were always under pressure to make sure the trips were a success. From Kissinger's trips, the Chinese learned they could gain considerable leverage by merely hinting to the press that a visit might "fail."

Secretary of State George Shultz seems to have mastered the Chinese tactic of forcing the other side to show its hand first—then exploiting its fear of failure. In recounting the American delegation's trip to New Delhi for Indira Gandhi's funeral, Daniel Patrick Moynihan described Shultz's skill: "[He] asked Vice Premier Yao Yilin of the People's Republic of China about his views of the region. The vice premier replied he would be interested in the secretary's views. This exchange was repeated until the appointed time of departure."[1]

Of course, in commercial negotiations such a strategy is inappropriate—especially if the ultimate goal is a business contract. But the executive should remember that Chinese businesspeople will play their cards close to the vest—even while insisting that visitors show their hands. Many U.S. executives report that—as a way of trying to pry out secrets—the Chinese have revealed information on competitors. Japanese trading companies avoid this problem with the Chinese by refusing to bid against each other.

Shadowboxing

Once negotiations begin, the Chinese seem passive. They simply ask questions, probe for information, and conceal any eagerness they may feel. They are wary of showing enthusiasm—an attitude that contrasts sharply with the American salesperson's excitement at the mere prospect of a deal. One U.S. aircraft parts supplier reports he was shocked to realize in retrospect that as the Chinese became more restrained, he became more energized—until he promised more than he could deliver.

During this phase, negotiators have learned to listen carefully because the Chinese often give subtle hints about their requirements for reaching an agreement. A plastics company executive believes that if he had heeded early Chinese signals he would have saved his company nearly a year's delay in setting up the joint venture. He was so absorbed with making points that he missed the hints they gave.

At times, the Chinese seem to become obsessed with a particular detail. It is important to remember that they may not really place great importance on it; they may be stalling. In fact, delaying things may be a necessity, not a tactic. They don't want to admit their difficulty in coordinating decisions, so they take up time with false questions. In the midst of serious negotiations, for example, the Chinese may suddenly suggest that the Americans take a break for some sight-seeing.

Various people's reports attest to the reality of this shadowboxing. Apparent sticking points can disappear once an agreement is reached. One

American importer of rare metals first haggled over prices, but reported that a year after the contract was signed the Chinese spontaneously offered new prices that were more favorable than those he had originally sought—because of changes in the exchange rate.

The Chinese use time shrewdly. If they sense that businesspeople are in a hurry to leave China, they may slow down negotiations and turn the deadline to their advantage. When China first opened up, some foreign executives thought they would have to hang their heads in shame if they left China without an agreement. Now many Americans are comfortable going home without a deal rather than settling on Chinese terms.

Ultimately, of course, this reaction serves little commercial purpose. Rather, executives should establish a clear understanding with the Chinese about the amount of time available and, most important, negotiate a fallback arrangement if they cannot reach agreement within the first time period. A West Coast lawyer follows the practice of beginning discussions by telling the Chinese exactly when he will be leaving and how long it will be before he can return.

These timetables can also change unexpectedly as Chinese passivity gives way to apparent impatience. Suddenly they want to reach agreement. They forget issues that were major obstacles and suggest that everything is in order and all further problems can be worked out.

This switch has surprised many U.S. businesspeople because it comes without any hint that a settlement is imminent. The two parties have different concepts of how an agreement is reached. Americans believe it follows a process of give-and-take that culminates when both sides have maximized their position. Chinese negotiators see an agreement more as a pledge from both sides. They believe a bond is sealed from the point when each side works out the benefits it will receive. An agreement binds the parties in a common endeavor wherein each side will make continuing demands on the other.

U.S. executives usually find that the Chinese are quick to talk of friendship and ready on short acquaintance to call them old friends. In the Chinese culture, all friends are "old friends" and what may seem to Americans as mere conviviality is to the Chinese an essential negotiating element. The Chinese can make heavy demands on friends and place few limits on how they use friendships to material advantage.

A subtle but profound difference in the way the two sides view friendships can have a strong effect on business negotiations. The Chinese place great importance on objective considerations and little on feelings. For example, they believe people from the same town, or same school, or the same organization should act as friends even if they don't know each

1 Daniel Patrick Moynihan,
"Indira Gandhi and Democracy,"
Freedom at Issue,
May-June 1985, p. 18.

other well. Morever, they expect the person who is better off to be always generous. They establish a bond so that they can ask for repeated favors and also so they can suggest that the partner who is not forthcoming is not living up to the spirit of their friendship. Americans see friendships as built on a natural give-and-take.

I am not surprised about the complaints of many U.S. executives that the Chinese fail to reciprocate friendship. American universities making scholarly exchanges with the Chinese are often irritated because they seem to provide a lot without getting much in return – scholarly aid, if you will, rather than exchange. The Chinese, however, would be offended if they heard this; they acknowledge the Americans' prestige simply by entering into the relationship. Americans doubt the cash value of prestige whereas the Chinese see it as a goal.

What the Chinese neglect in terms of reciprocity, however, they more than match in loyalty. They not only keep their commitments but they also assume that any positive relationship can be permanent. A good example of this is the number of Chinese who have tried to reestablish pre-1949 ties with U.S. companies and individuals – as though nothing had happened in the intervening years.

In business dealings, Chinese feelings about reciprocity surface most sharply in discussions of technology transfer. The Chinese want to gain access to advanced technologies – they believe that although their country missed out on the first two industrial revolutions, it can get in on the start of the third, the information revolution. But they don't appreciate proprietary rights. They believe that knowledge should belong to everyone; those who have technical knowledge should share it. They don't appreciate how much it costs to produce technologies, a fact that is evident in the way they wastefully try to reverse-engineer products – buying a model, then trying to replicate it through inefficient, cottage-industry methods.

Pursuing goals

The Chinese assume – wrongly – that they can solve most of their modernization problems with more advanced science and technology. A frequent stumbling block in negotiations has been specification of the technology a foreign partner would bring to the joint venture. The problem is more serious than one might assume because China's difficulties have more to do with poor business management than with lack of technology.

In any contract, management arrangements are hard to pin down. Because the Chinese generally provide almost all the employees, U.S. business-people must make certain that the deal contains satisfactory management arrangements. If the Chinese have done poorly in an industry without a foreign partner, this pattern may continue in a partnership, even with advanced technologies. Agreements should include arrangements for training management, not just teaching technical or engineering skills.

Negotiations over the costs of such training can be sticky. In some of the hotel deals, the Chinese not only discounted the costs of training but were also quick to suggest that Americans absorb training costs, including high overhead expenses like medical care and housing.

The Chinese also want to do business with the "best" foreign companies. They place a high value on quality and status, and they often suspect they are not getting the best – a concern that aggravates an already strong anxiety about getting cheated. Although the latest technologies may not always be the most appropriate, the Chinese cannot suppress their suspicion that foreign companies mistreat them when they try to sell them equipment that the Chinese sense is not the most advanced.

This fear stems from memories of past ill-treatment by foreigners and from a rural tradition holding that all transactions produce a winner and a loser. The fear is exacerbated by the anxieties of Chinese negotiators that their superiors may accuse them of making bad deals. Plant managers have far greater freedom than in the past, but their careers are still vulnerable to changes in the political currents.

Because of such Chinese concerns, little-known foreign companies have trouble in selling themselves. If they play up their competitive advantages, the Chinese may suspect them of boasting; if they are too modest, the Chinese will dismiss them as not being the best. In American negotiations, frankness is a virtue; it is considered wise to admit failings. The Chinese believe that if you admit to one weakness, you are probably covering up even greater ones.

The American goal is a binding agreement secured by a stable and enduring legal system, a contract with all the power and mystique we associate with the law. The Chinese see stability not in the power of the law but in the strength of human relationships. A contract establishes what is essentially a personal relationship. Although the Chinese are now developing a more institutionalized legal system, their culture still reflects a philosophy that governance is more by people than by laws.

Even the Chinese who are in charge of a state company may have very limited and uncertain authority and may want to settle for a tacit rather than a written understanding. Even with considerable decentralization, managers remain hemmed in by the system and often have little sense of the boundaries of their authority.

This problem of limited authority becomes particularly acute when Americans expect the kind of commitments they get in other countries. China's inadequate infrastructure means that Chinese negotiators cannot make firm guarantees on matters that depend on, say, the system of transportation or supplies of energy.

How to handle them

Although I do not intend to outline a counterstrategy for executives going into a negotiation with the Chinese, I would like to summarize my thoughts as a list of do's and don'ts in dealing with them:

1   Always be yourself. While you should be sensitive to Chinese cultural practices, you must never believe you can master their ways.

2   Be patient, both in the actual negotiations and in designing an overall strategy. Impatience not only leaves you vulnerable to manipulation but also produces agreements that can result in misunderstandings later and compromise your access to China.

3   Recognize that you cannot even guess at the shape of China's future development. Her success could take various forms, each good for China but each with different implications for different American businesses.

4   Accept that you cannot define or govern your Chinese company with any formal contract. Learn to shape it through the human relationships established through the negotiations and actual conduct of the business.

5   Be prepared for misunderstandings and avoid recriminations over them. Although the Chinese often seem uninhibited in exploiting American mistakes, they are just as likely to be thin-skinned and quick to take offense. China's recent foreign relations are full of examples of Beijing having bitter fallings-out with former allies.

6   Accept the Chinese offer of friendship in the spirit in which it is extended. The relationship can have a practical and materialistic as well as a sentimental dimension. Understand that even though the Chinese may not seem as sensitive to considerations of reciprocity as Westerners or the Japanese, they place much value on loyalty and they will uphold their side of any bargain even as they try to get further concessions. ▽

Reprint 86410

Ming dynasty business contract

Wherever a money economy prevails, commercial transactions such as buying and selling, borrowing money, and renting houses are important parts of people's daily lives. Because most economic relations potentially involve conflicts of interest, they need to be regulated by well-understood traditions, written agreements, or both. By the T'ang dynasty [618-907 A.D.], contracts seem to have been in wide use in China, and thereafter even illiterate peasants realized the importance of having a piece of paper to prove the original terms of an agreement. Private financial agreements could be drawn up by any two individuals, usually with the aid of a mediator or a witness. Experts in legal matters were not normally consulted, but to ensure that most foreseeable problems had been dealt with, people could consult sample contracts.

Here is a blank contract taken from a late Ming [dynasty 1368-1644 A.D.] reference book.... Most such contracts and bills of sale state that the transaction was legal and had not been coerced. They also carefully specify who is responsible if anything goes wrong. Very often the weaker party (the man seeking to borrow money, be hired, sell his child, and so on) clearly accepts the brunt of the responsibility should anything unexpected happen. Such economic relations surely must have also shaped social relations.

Sample contract for forming a business partnership

The undersigned, _____ and _____, having observed that partnerships bring profit and enterprise brings success, have agreed to pool their capital for profit. As witnessed by a mediator, _____, they have each contributed _____ as capital, and will cooperate sincerely in their business venture. The profit yielded will be divided between them each year to provide for their families. The capital will remain untouched to serve as the fountainhead of the business. Each individual will take care of his own personal expenses and not draw from the capital, nor should business and private expenditures be in any way mixed in bookkeeping. The two parties have taken an oath by drinking blood-wine to work together in harmony and share both profits and losses. They will not disagree, feud, or seek separate profits. The party that breaks this contract will be persecuted by gods and men alike.

This contract is drawn up in two copies as evidence of the agreement.

From
Chinese Civilization and Society: A Sourcebook
ed. Patricia Buckley Ebrey
Copyright © 1981 by
The Free Press
A Division of Macmillan
Publishing Co., Inc.
Reprinted by permission

Foreign ownership: when hosts change the rules

Dennis J. Encarnation and Sushil Vachani

Canny guests play the new game and turn equity losses into business opportunities

Legislation that requires multinational corporations to dilute their equity in overseas subsidiaries will never be welcome on the fortieth floor. At best it heralds shared ownership and perhaps control; at worst it can mean a reluctant departure from the country. Yet the consequences of such legislation are often surprisingly favorable, as this study makes clear. New product lines and markets, risk diversification, and higher earnings are among the benefits MNCs operating in India enjoyed in the wake of that country's "hostile" equity laws.

They did so, in large part, because their managers were prepared to be flexible – and imaginative – in responding to the government's demands. Some, for example, negotiated for manufacturing licenses and other valuable permits in exchange for "Indianization." Others increased exports or introduced high-technology products and thereby fostered the government's economic plans. But whatever strategies they chose, these executives signaled their willingness to strike a balance between their companies' goals and those of their host. And in the end, that may be the most important lesson their experiences teach.

Mr. Encarnation is assistant professor at the Harvard Business School, where he teaches courses in international business and business-government relations. His book, Bargaining in India's Uneasy Triangle, *is forthcoming.*

Mr. Vachani of the Boston Consulting Group has worked in India as a manager in both MNCs and local enterprises.

Illustration by Gustav Szabo.

Political pressure for national control of multinational corporations is on the rise, and few MNCs are unaffected. Whether the company under duress is Unilever in Canada, Coca-Cola in India, IBM in France, or Ford in Mexico, the story remains the same. Governments of every political stripe are vying for greater domestic ownership of foreign operations within their borders.

Constraints on foreign ownership have taken many forms: Canada's former Foreign Investment Review Act, France's nationalization schemes, Korea's foreign remittance regulations, and "Mexicanization" programs with correlates throughout the world. But even though these policies differ, common features are discernible, particularly when it comes to exemptions. In general, the greater the level of exports, R&D expenditures, foreign exchange savings, and high technology associated with a project, the greater the probability that prohibitions on majority foreign holdings can be relaxed. Yet even then, governments increasingly insist on the diminution of foreign holdings over a specified period or proscribe majority foreign participation in new projects.

In responding to demands for equity dilution, MNCs have a range of strategic options from which to choose, in part because administrative discretion in implementing regulations provides leeway for negotiation. But this flexibility is not always apparent to managers at the parent's headquarters or at the subsidiary. As a result, many companies fail to turn a potentially adverse situation to their competitive advantage.

Nowhere is the regulation of foreign equity participation more encompassing – and, some would say, more onerous – than in India, the focus of our study (see insert). Yet the constraints MNCs face there are representative of those they encounter elsewhere. Focusing on corporate responses to India's equity regulations thus teaches lessons that managers throughout the world can apply.

A portfolio of responses

India's Foreign Exchange Regulation Act, or FERA, of 1973 restricts foreign equity participation in local operations to 40%. As in other countries, however, several exemptions can apply. If the company operates in high-priority industries that require "sophisticated technology," for example, or exports a "significant proportion" of output, officials may grant an exemption of up to 74%. And if the company exports its entire output, 100% foreign equity may be allowed. But intense negotiations between country managers and government regulators invariably precede extension of these exemptions.

India's rationale for regulating foreign investment this way is similar to that found elsewhere. The perceived economic benefits that flow from retaining more corporate earnings and the managerial control that presumably would follow a change in ownership are among the chief arguments for forced equity dilutions. In addition, such regulation responds to pressure from local competitors who invoke nationalistic sentiment to support their claims on the government.

Managers compelled to reduce foreign equity holdings have at least four options: strict compliance, exit, negotiation, and preemptive action.

Option 1:
Follow the law to the letter

Companies that sought to maintain existing operations typically sold a majority of their foreign shares to local investors and kept total equity constant. This strategy allowed Colgate-Palmolive (India) to continue producing and marketing a low-technology product line, toothpaste, for which local substitutes existed. Without reclassification as an Indian-owned company, Colgate could not continue to operate in India. By diluting its foreign equity to 40%, it officially became an Indian company and could thereby maintain its dominant position in a profitable and growing market, well protected by entry barriers. (By law, an "Indian" company is one in which the foreign equity share is 40% or less.)

Option 2:
Leave the country

As the widely publicized divestitures of IBM and Coca-Cola illustrate, Indian local ownership requirements forced some companies to leave the country during the late 1970s. Still, exit was not the managers' first choice at any of these companies. Rather, the decision followed a long process of negotiation with government agencies. Consider what happened in the computer industry.

Before 1977, IBM, two other multinationals, and an Indian government-owned company battled for an expanded role in the Indian market. To maintain its competitive advantage, IBM tried to apply FERA selectively. It offered to establish two separate companies: one, a wholly foreign-owned branch for marketing, maintaining, and manufacturing export items; the other, a 40% foreign-owned affiliate to handle data center operations in India. Shares in the affiliate would be widely distributed locally.

Burroughs, a relative newcomer to the Indian market, offered an alternative, proposing to set up a joint venture with an Indian company controlled by the country's second largest business conglomerate, Tata. British-owned International Computer also proposed to set up a minority foreign-owned joint venture with a large-scale private Indian manufacturer, Bharat Electronics. In opposition, the government-owned Electronics Corporation urged that all three foreign companies be shut out of the market, which it alone should dominate.

The government rejected both the Electronics Corporation and IBM proposals. It allowed multinationals to operate in the country but it insisted on equity dilution for manufacturing operations. Burroughs and International Computer decided to go ahead with their plans, while IBM chose to leave the country. Presumably IBM's management thought it would lose more by setting a precedent for shared control with local partners than it could gain from continued operations under the new rules. IBM therefore had few options.

Option 3:
Negotiate under the law

For some MNCs, the equity dilution requirement became an opportunity to grow and diversify because their managers used it as a negotiating tool to raise funds, obtain government licenses, and win approval for new product lines.

Issuing fresh equity exclusively to local investors and leaving the absolute number of shares held by the parent constant was the most common dilution scheme. In this way, Purolator, Ciba-Geigy, and other MNCs used dilution to raise funds for expansion. Ciba-Geigy's dilution scheme, for example, increased the total equity base of its subsidiary, Hindustan Ciba-Geigy, by 27% to $17.7 million. The funds from the new equity, which sold at 40% over book value, contributed nearly one-third of the total capital necessary to undertake expansion in 1983 and 1984.

Ciba-Geigy's management also used equity dilution as a lever to expand its product lines. By law the company only had to reduce its equity in Hindustan Ciba-Geigy from 65% to 51% since it operated in a high-technology industry. Ciba-Geigy volunteered to dilute its equity to 40%, however, so that its subsidiary could benefit from classification as an Indian company. In return, the company was free to produce pharmaceutical formulations valued at ten times the sale of its bulk drugs, or twice the manufacturing capacity permitted non-Indian producers. Thus Hindustan Ciba-Geigy's dilution strategy cleared the way for it to double its pharmaceutical sales.

Like Ciba-Geigy, Chesebrough-Pond's reduced its holdings in its wholly owned branch to 40% by issuing new equity exclusively to Indian investors. Three production and marketing changes followed this infusion of new capital in its subsidiary, Pond's (India). First, its manufacturing operation expanded from one plant to four in the next five years. Because these factories were located in backward regions, where the government encouraged investment through tax holidays, subsidized loans, and other incentives, the subsidiary's effective tax rates and cost of capital plummeted. Second, in those same five years, the company stopped relying exclusively on the Indian domestic market and began exporting 30% of its sales. Third, by 1983, the company was poised to diversify its product line by introducing clinical thermometers destined for the U.S. market.

As Ciba-Geigy's experience indicates, negotiations over equity dilution are invariably linked to negotiations over other regulatory policies—of which India has many. Indeed, India's regulatory regime has been euphemistically called the "license-cum-permit Raj" to highlight the myriad directorates, departments, secretariats, and ministries whose approval must be secured for operations to proceed. Yet even these obstacles may beget opportunities for MNCs.

For example, India's industrial licensing system prohibits a company from expanding capacity beyond approved limits or entering new product lines or markets without permission. Yet if a company can secure a license previously denied, the system turns around: the new license serves as an entry barrier to domestic competitors, just as India's import restrictions serve as barriers to foreign competition. So if management can secure an industrial license as a negotiating concession, the benefits derived from expansion and diversification may offset the costs of dilution to the parent corporation.

Moving from expansion to diversification was a common strategy. Both steps often occurred

---

A note on the research

To explore the range of responses available to managements under pressure to dilute their equity ownership in local subsidiaries, we studied 12 companies operating in India during the late 1970s. Each of these MNCs—Unilever, Purolator, Massey-Ferguson, Maremont, IBM, Cummins Engine, Colgate-Palmolive, Coca-Cola, Ciba-Geigy, Chesebrough-Pond's, Burroughs, and British-American Tobacco—faced similar demands in other countries. And each has had to develop a strategy for meeting this threat worldwide. Our analysis draws on the companies' public financial documents as well as interviews with corporate executives and Indian government officials. These interviews took place in three stages, beginning in 1977 and ending in 1983.

---

simultaneously. Consider the most ambitious equity dilution scheme undertaken in India, a strategy devised by Gabriel India Limited, a subsidiary of Gabriel International (Panama) and, by merger, the Maremont Corporation (USA).

Gabriel India was one of the country's largest manufacturers of shock absorbers even before equity dilution. When it agreed in 1978 to reduce its foreign stake from 50% to 39%, the government granted the company licenses to double production of shock absorbers. In addition, the company received permission to diversify into engine bearings with the technological collaboration of a new American partner, Federal Mogul.

Federal Mogul made several demands, including an equity position in a recapitalized Gabriel India, that countered regulations. It also insisted that Gabriel India remit dividends during the new partnership's first year, even though none of its earnings would come from manufacturing bearings. Finally, Federal Mogul demanded that royalties and technical fees be paid sooner and at higher rates than normally permitted. After heated negotiations, the government consented to all of Federal Mogul's demands—in exchange for equity dilution of Gabriel India and larger output of two products in chronically short supply.

To finance this investment and dilute foreign holdings, Gabriel India nearly doubled its equity to $2.6 million, through a complex series of transactions. By selling fresh equity to Federal Mogul and local investors, the company generated nearly one-fifth of the capital needed for expansion. Simultaneously, Gabriel International and its original Indian partner sold existing shares to government-run financial institutions. These institutions, in turn, financed the remaining new investment through a mix of commercial and concessional loans, supplemented by government subsidies. When the dust settled, Indian investors held 61% of Gabriel India, Gabriel International held 25%, and Federal Mogul held 14%.

Option 4:
Take preemptive action

Unlike the companies described so far, some MNCs initiated defensive strategies, such as preemptive diversification, phased "Indianization," and joint partnerships, well before FERA's final passage. Still others, like Cummins Engine, deflected political pressure by continuously updating their technology and bringing in valuable foreign exchange through exports.

Preemptive diversification. Hindustan Lever developed a four-pronged strategy to avoid equity dilution. That strategy allowed it to retain majority ownership of a subsidiary whose business portfolio differed from its own. At the core of this strategy were sustained efforts to increase high-technology production and export sales. First, during the 1970s, management added basic chemicals to the detergents, soaps, and other consumer goods that made up its product lines. This addition both reflected the high priority given such manufacture by the government and fit Hindustan Lever's plan for backward integration. Then, in 1983, the company further increased the proportion of high technology in its business portfolio by selling its food business to a second Unilever subsidiary, Lipton India.

Local R&D efforts made up the third feature of Hindustan Lever's high-technology strategy. As a result of these R&D investments, products like detergent could be classified as "high technology." Further, the company's research facility, one of the largest in India's private sector, found ways to substitute locally abundant oils for imported tallow in the manufacture of high-quality soaps. This substitution saved scarce foreign exchange, another government priority.

The fourth prong of Hindustan Lever's strategy also focused on foreign exchange. To boost earnings, the government offered incentives to large companies that would establish export houses as channels for smaller manufacturers unable to export on their own. Hindustan Lever, already a licensed export house selling a variety of other companies' products overseas, took steps to increase the proportion of exports in its sales. Export sales then grew rapidly, more than tripling in five years to reach $62 million in 1982. In that year, the government decided to allow Unilever to retain its majority ownership of Hindustan Lever since 60% of the subsidiary's activities generated foreign exchange, involved high technology, or operated in high-priority sectors.

Phased Indianization. At ITC, a subsidiary of the British-American Tobacco Company, the quest for new capital and businesses entailed a strategy of phased Indianization. During the late 1960s, ITC's management realized that the government was unlikely to grant majority foreign ownership rights for a product—cigarettes—that was closely tied to agriculture, required little new technology or large capital investments, and had minuscule prospects for export. Because internal and foreign funds for diversification were limited and government licenses were increasingly reserved for Indian companies, management chose to look for new opportunities through voluntary divestment.

Through sale of fresh equity and existing stock, the company reduced its foreign ownership from 94% in 1968 to 75% in 1969, 60% in 1974 (following FERA), and 40% in 1976. Moves to diversify ITC's business accompanied each of these divestments. In 1971, the company began to export products, ranging from frozen shrimp to hand tools to handwoven carpets, that it did not manufacture. By 1973, it had obtained government approval to enter the hotel business (ten years later owning 3 luxury hotels and managing a chain of 18 others). And in 1976, it decided to promote a capital-intensive paperboard venture. By 1982, ITC had diversified in two important ways: from manufacturing to service industries and from local marketing of a single product to exporting various products.

Joint partnerships. For another group of companies, neither diversification nor dilution was necessary even after FERA's passage. These multinationals already satisfied its requirements because they either continuously updated technology in a politically salient industry or earned sufficient foreign exchange. After 1973, the principal strategy of such joint ventures as Kirloskar-Cummins, Tata-Burroughs, and TAFE (a subsidiary of Massey-Ferguson) was to maintain existing operations. The 50% share of equity held by Cummins Engine, the 50% share held by Burroughs, and the 49% share held by Massey-Ferguson were secure provided that the technological content of the products remained high and export sales did not decline.

Kirloskar-Cummins, for example, kept on adding larger horsepower products to its line of sophisticated diesel engines. Because it was the only producer of one particular engine, the Cummins subsidiary also had a secure, albeit small, export market. Burroughs likewise staved off equity dilution pressure through its high-technology products and growing computer-software export sales. (Burroughs's wholly owned subsidiary in the Santa Cruz Export Processing Zone contributed significantly to India's burgeoning sales of labor-intensive software design and data-entry operations to overseas clients.)

Reaping the benefits

Companies that negotiated dilution packages after FERA was enacted or took preemptive action before its passage were able to retain majority ownership or at least maintain managerial control, diversify risk, and ultimately raise the profits of the parent or the subsidiary.

Retaining majority ownership

A few MNCs succeeded in keeping majority ownership of their subsidiaries even after FERA's passage. Although all met at least one of the act's criteria for exemption, what usually tipped the scale was the parent's supply of high technology in a favored industry. Some of these MNCs had earlier formed joint partnerships with Indian companies. Occasionally, however, the high technology was homegrown by country managers, such as those at Hindustan Lever, who invested heavily in local R&D.

Maintaining managerial control

Majority ownership is only one means of exercising control, as executives in India long ago recognized. In each divestiture cited, foreign equity holdings were reduced without compromising MNC control over the subsidiary. When fresh equity was issued to local investors (the most common financial response) or existing foreign shares were sold, the equity was dispersed widely among many individual shareholders, each with a small holding. In 1980, for example, 89,000 Indians held Hindustan Lever's stock. Smaller MNCs were similarly able to maintain control: more than 11,000 Indian nationals owned 57% of Pond's (India) after the parent reduced its share to 40%.

In all these cases, large blocks of shares were seldom, if ever, sold to a single private Indian enterprise. The only big institutional buyers were public sector financial agencies—often the largest single Indian shareholders after dilution. And even they were reluctant to intervene in day-to-day operations, generally deferring to managers installed by the MNC. In this way, managerial control remained unchanged after dilution.

Diversifying risk

Subsidiaries and parents that maintained control also benefited by diversifying the risks of operation. For example, MNCs that reduced their foreign holdings to 40% were assured "national treatment" under the law. Pond's (India) was thereby allowed to build new plants to expand production; Gabriel India could diversify into an industry protected by high technological entry barriers; and ITC could enter a business in which its parent had no experience. Through these moves, the MNCs diversified the risks associated with narrow product lines, limited production facilities, and restricted markets. Even more important, the government licenses they secured let them hurdle entry barriers that kept out potential competitors, foreign and domestic.

Increasing profits

The benefits of retained ownership and control show up on the income statement of the parent, the subsidiary, or both. Even the simplest response to FERA, complying with the letter of the law to maintain operations, yielded benefits for Colgate-Palmolive (India), which thereby retained its 50% to 60% share of a fast-growing, highly protected market. By 1982, the subsidiary's revenues had reached $77.6 million, having grown along with net worth at an annual rate of 18% since 1973. During the same period, after-tax profits increased 11% per annum and dividends rose 9%. Dilution of foreign equity in 1978 did, however, depress the level of dividends allotted to the parent in the next few years. But pretax dividends in the four years after dilution, plus pretax value of the sale of equity, exceeded the parent's pretax receipts in the four years preceding dilution by roughly 25%. Moreover, the parent's share in the subsidiary's net worth grew at an annual rate of nearly 8% between 1973 and 1982.

The benefits of negotiation were even more impressive for companies that linked equity dilution to expansion. At the recapitalized and diversified Pond's (India), for instance, after-tax profits grew 57% annually, sales grew 27%, and dividends to the parent grew 49% in the first four years after the company's legal status changed from branch to subsidiary. The increase in profits over sales reflected local management's effective use of tax holidays, subsidized credit, and other incentives available through negotiation with government agencies seeking investment in underdeveloped regions. It is unlikely that this subsidiary would have been allowed to diversify and grow at rates anywhere near as high without diluting its equity.

Preemptive strategies designed to increase the parent's bargaining power yielded similar financial results. By 1982, two years after equity dilution, Hindustan Lever could report that after-tax profits had reached $22.2 million, having grown at an annual rate of 24% over the previous nine years, more than double the rate of inflation. During the same period, sales and dividends rose 16% and 12% respectively. By diversifying into new products and markets, Hindustan Lever not only warded off further equity dilution but also reaped greater financial rewards.

Earnings at companies that avoided equity dilution altogether also grew unimpeded after FERA's passage. Kirloskar-Cummins secured several new licenses for capacity expansion and technological collaboration between 1973 and 1982. During that period, after-tax profits rose at a compound annual rate of 39% to $8.2 million, while revenues rose 24% to $89.5 million. Dividends to the parent grew significantly too, rising 25% annually to reach $825,000 by 1982. The parent's earnings were also boosted by technical fees, which grew at a compound annual rate of 23% to $1 million in 1982.

Limits to choice

While creative responses to forced equity dilution can yield profitable results, practical considerations and constraints often deny managers the luxury of choosing freely from this portfolio. Factors that limit the range of available options include: the implications of setting a precedent, the MNC's decision-making structure, the level of bargaining power, the political environment, and management's attitudes.[1]

Precedent setting

Because a single government's actions can affect other parts of a company, few multinational managements can safely ignore the implications of business-government negotiations in any one country. First, in some cases, what matters to one government has a direct impact on the operation of subsidiaries elsewhere. Local-content legislation or minimum export requirements, for example, may force a multinational to reconfigure its international sourcing arrangements. IBM in India rejected both demands on the ground that they would disrupt its global operations.

Second, and probably more important from IBM's perspective, a decision in one country can set a precedent for demands from other governments. Even though Indian operations made up an insignificant part of IBM's global activities, it devoted a great deal of management time to the issue of equity dilution. As a compromise, IBM finally offered to reduce its ownership of the local sales operations to 40%. But it would not budge from its corporate policy of 100% ownership of manufacturing subsidiaries. And when this proved unacceptable, IBM withdrew rather than yield to pressure that could undermine its policies elsewhere. Soon thereafter, the company left Nigeria over the same issue.

IBM was not alone in trying to keep important corporate policies intact. Coca-Cola left India (and other countries) to avoid disclosing its famed formula to a local partner. And petroleum and mining companies must likewise consider the wider implications of their negotiations, lest they grant one country concessions that all may demand.

Centralized decision making

MNCs deeply concerned about precedents usually keep decision making centralized. IBM, for example, gave authority for all equity dilution decisions to its Corporate Management Committee, consisting of the company's top five executives. Coca-Cola adopted a similar approach. These decisions were not made lightly because centralization almost completely disenfranchises subsidiary or other front-line managers responsible for the unit's profits, knowledge of local conditions, and day-to-day management tasks. For certain MNCs, however, larger corporate strategic issues, such as protecting intangible assets, make centralized control essential.

Other companies try to coordinate business-government negotiations with less centralized decision-making structures. Like IBM, pharmaceutical companies know that governments are almost certain to have a close interest in their industry and its activities. So these companies often try to apply one subsidiary's experience to another to maintain important corporate policies, including majority ownership. (Given the proprietary nature of technology, patents, and trademarks, drug companies generally try to

1 For a discussion of precedents and centralized decision making, see Amir Mahini and Louis T. Wells, Jr., "Managing Government Relations in Multinational Enterprises," paper presented at the Colloquium on Competition in Global Industries, Harvard Business School, April 1984.

2 For a summary of the literature from which these findings are drawn, see Dennis J. Encarnation and Louis T. Wells, Jr., "Competitive Strategies in Global Industries: A View from the Host Country," paper presented at the Colloquium on Competition in Global Industries, Harvard Business School, April 1984.

maintain majority equity holdings in their foreign subsidiaries.)

For these reasons, Ciba-Geigy's corporate management was surprised by the recommendation of its Indian subsidiary that it voluntarily reduce its foreign equity, not to the 51% approved by the Indian government but to 40%. To prevail, local management had to demonstrate that the new avenues for higher profits resulting from classification as an Indian company justified dilution of foreign equity in a subsidiary already generating impressive earnings from existing operations.

The degree of autonomy accorded local managers, of course, differs greatly, even among MNCs engaged in similar businesses. The U.S. headquarters of Colgate-Palmolive controls decision making tightly, and it would be unlikely to allow its subsidiaries to diversify into unfamiliar product lines. Decision making at Unilever is decentralized, and Hindustan Lever's managers (encouraged by the Indian government) are able to choose from a wider range of strategic options and thereby introduce new product lines.

Bargaining power

IBM's ability to hold the Indian government at bay for more than a decade reflects the strength of its bargaining position. Yet the IBM story also reminds us that a corporate nonnegotiation policy cannot remain intact forever. Agreements reached at the preinvestment stage, when a company's bargaining position is usually strongest, will become obsolete over time.

The greater an MNC's bargaining power, the less its need to respond to government demands. In general, a foreign company's bargaining power is likely to increase if it:

Exports a large part of its output and can control the market downstream from the production site.

Uses factors of production, such as unskilled labor, that can be easily substituted across countries.

Occupies a monopolistic or dominant oligopolistic position in the industry.

Uses high technology that has few substitute sources.

Produces highly differentiated products that require large marketing or R&D expenditures.

Requires no capital-intensive facilities expenditures that once in place are difficult to liquidate or move.[2]

These factors are not immutable. As we have seen, Unilever's local management hiked the company's bargaining power by transforming a low-technology, domestic producer of limited consumer goods into an exporting, R&D-intensive, high-technology diversified company. But to do this, management had to avoid relying on old bargains that time and events were eroding.

Political environment

All such strategies could be for naught, of course, given the vicissitudes of politics. IBM, for example, suffered from several political liabilities. It had a high profile; it was identified as a U.S. company at a time when relations were strained; and in the view of the new government that came to power suddenly in 1977 it was closely associated with the earlier Gandhi regime. Moreover, party stalwarts used the case as a litmus test of policy changes and pressed the new government to penalize IBM for its violations of FERA. Still, the new government acted only after it was sure that substitute products were readily available. Much the same could be said for Coca-Cola. In both cases, the political environment probably exacerbated other constraints noted previously.

As IBM's experience suggests, the political environment limits managements' options in important ways. Yet politics alone is not enough to explain corporate choices. Burroughs was one of several U.S. companies that stayed in India after IBM left; indeed, it took advantage of that departure. Other companies, like Unilever, Colgate-Palmolive, and Chesebrough-Pond's, also had strong domestic competitors who applied political pressure to oust them from markets where foreign ownership was harder to justify.

Management's attitudes

Finally, executives' own spectacles can limit the options they perceive. In many cases, overseas managers receive their assignments because of their skills in marketing, production, or other functional areas. Experience in government relations is rarely part of their background, especially if they have been transferred from domestic operations in the United States. Further, without special effort from higher up, the managers often have little chance to learn from their peers' experience in other countries.

Lacking experience or shared information, managers commonly assume that government, virtually by definition, impedes private business. And the "license-cum-permit Raj" that is India only reinforces this view. Yet to undertake the creative responses we have outlined, managers had to overcome these biases. Otherwise they could not have converted government constraints into business assets.

Ironically, even success can constrain a company's responses, unless its management guards against the inertia bred by good performance. At Ciba-Geigy, for instance, the reasons for Indianization would not have been obvious to headquarters, since its government-approved operation was already very profitable. But local management saw opportunities in the FERA regulations and persuaded the parent to pursue them with even more profitable results for all.

Lessons for managers

The experiences of MNCs in India teach important lessons for managers worldwide who must respond to host country regulatory policies:

Look at the range of strategic possibilities. The 12 MNCs that we studied unequivocally show that no single strategy works best in a single country or even a single industry. And we can assume that the same conclusion holds true across countries as well. To beat the competition, both parent and subsidiary managements must assess the full portfolio of responses. If you don't, your competitor may. In India, it has proved difficult for Colgate-Palmolive to move into detergent, a product it markets worldwide, partly as a result of Unilever's aggressive marketing and R&D strategy.

Use the law to further your own ends. Unilever, Chesebrough-Pond's, and Gabriel India were among the companies that turned adversity into opportunity. By satisfying government demands, such companies availed themselves of government concessions —new licenses to expand or diversify, subsidized loans, and tariff protection. As a result, they transcended some barriers erected by the government controls and also reduced their cost of capital. Other competitors, unable to obtain similar concessions, faced higher entry barriers than these multinationals. Moreover, the additional earnings and risk diversification offset the costs to the parent of complying with the regulations. In short, these MNCs exploited the opportunities that flow from administrative discretion in implementing regulatory and incentive policies.

Create future bargaining chips. By linking regulations to concessions, many of these companies reversed the process of obsolescence that inevitably afflicts negotiated settlements. Unilever, for example, could no longer be treated like any other foreign producer of mass consumer goods once it had reconfigured its operations in response to FERA. Rather, its technology and exports were now critical to "self-reliant development"–the byword of India and many other countries. Before the government can again demand that Unilever reduce its majority foreign holdings, substitutes for its products and alternatives to its operations must materialize. But in the meantime, Unilever is seen as a good corporate citizen, and it will be in an even better negotiating position the next time around.

Anticipate government policy changes. Building bargaining chips takes time. Of the 12 MNCs we examined, ITC and others that took the initiative had greater freedom to shape their operations than those who waited to act until after FERA had passed. Moreover, some strategies like phased Indianization and preemptive diversification work better when management still has greater control over the timetables for equity dilution, capital infusion, new investment, and so on. Often, government agencies grant special consideration to companies that act early, viewing them as good corporate citizens. And finally, time is critical to bring about changes in the local subsidiary and between the subsidiary and its parent. Internal negotiations are often as crucial as negotiations between the company and the government, and the time they require can best be bought by anticipating government action.

Listen to your country managers. Local managers deserve top management's ear for several reasons. They are likely to know when issues are arising, they understand the political environment better, and they are more familiar with the intricacies of the law. Managers who have spent several years in a country may even know government leaders and other important officials.

Further, as the people likely to be most affected by the outcome of negotiations, country managers have a strong incentive to make recommendations that are beneficial to the subsidiary's interests. What is good for the subsidiary may not be good for the MNC as a whole, of course.

The dictum to obtain the country manager's advice does not mean that it must always be heeded. Yet the experience of these 12 companies suggests that it is the country manager who can best turn adversity into opportunity through creative responses in a hostile environment. ▽

Reprint 85507

READ THE FINE PRINT

REPRINTS
Telephone: 617-495-6192
Fax: 617-495-6985

Current and past articles
are available, as is an
annually updated index.
Discounts apply to
large-quantity purchases.

Please send orders to
HBR Reprints
Harvard Business School
Publishing Division
Boston, MA 02163.

HOW CAN *HARVARD BUSINESS REVIEW* ARTICLES WORK FOR YOU?

For years, we've printed a microscopically small notice on the editorial credits page of the *Harvard Business Review* alerting our readers to the availability of *HBR* articles.

Now we invite you to take a closer look at some of the many ways you can put this hard-working business tool to work for you.

IN THE CORPORATE CLASSROOM.

There's no more effective, or cost-effective, way to supplement your corporate training programs than in-depth, incisive *HBR* articles.

Affordable and accessible, it's no wonder hundreds of companies and consulting organizations use *HBR* articles as a centerpiece for management training.

IN-BOX INNOVATION.

Where do your company's movers and shakers get their big ideas? Many find the inspiration for innovation in the pages of *HBR*. They then share the wealth and spread the word by distributing *HBR* articles to company colleagues.

IN MARKETING AND SALES SUPPORT.

HBR articles are a substantive leave-behind to your sales calls. And they can add credibility to your direct mail campaigns. They demonstrate that your company is on the leading edge of business thinking.

CREATE CUSTOM ARTICLES.

If you want to pack even greater power in your punch, personalize *HBR* articles with your company's name or logo. And get the added benefit of putting your organization's name before your customers.

AND THERE ARE 500 MORE REASONS IN THE *HBR CATALOG*.

In all, the *Harvard Business Review Catalog* lists articles on over 500 different subjects. Plus, you'll find books and videos on subjects you need to know.

The catalog is yours for just $8.00. To order *HBR* articles or the *HBR Catalog* (No. 21019), call 617-495-6192. Please mention telephone order code 025A when placing your order. Or FAX us at 617-495-6985.

And start putting *HBR* articles to work for you.

**Harvard Business School
Publications**

Call 617-495-6192 to order the *HBR Catalog*.

(Prices and terms subject to change.)

YOU SAID: AND WE SAID:

❝Give us training tools that are relevant to our business...ones we can use *now.*❞

❝We need new cases that stimulate meaningful discussion.❞

❝It can't be a catalog of canned programs... everything we do is custom.❞

❝Make it a single source for up-to-date materials ...on the most current business topics.❞

❝Better yet if it's from a reputable business school. That adds credibility.❞

❝Introducing the Harvard Business School Publications Corporate Training and Development Catalog.❞

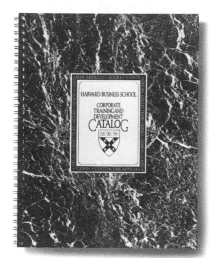

You asked for it. And now it's here.

The Harvard Business School Publications Corporate Training and Development Catalog is created exclusively for those who design and develop custom training programs.

It's filled cover-to-cover with valuable materials you can put to work on the spot. You'll find a comprehensive selection of cases, *Harvard Business Review* articles, videos, books, and more.

Our new catalog covers the critical management topics affecting corporations today, like Leadership, Quality, Global Business, Marketing, and Strategy, to name a few. And it's all organized, indexed, and cross-referenced to make it easy for you to find precisely what you need.

HOW TO ORDER.

To order by FAX, dial 617-495-6985. Or call 617-495-6192. Please mention telephone order code 132A. Or send this coupon with your credit card information to: HBS Publications Corporate Training and Development Catalog, Harvard Business School Publishing Division, Operations Department, Boston, MA 02163. **All orders must be prepaid.**

Order No.	Title	Qty. ×	Price +	Shipping* =	Total
39001	Catalog		$8		

Prices and terms subject to change.
For orders outside Continental U.S.: 20% for surface delivery. Allow 3-6 months. *Express Deliveries* billed at cost; all foreign orders not designating express delivery will be sent by surface mail.

☐ VISA ☐ American Express ☐ MasterCard

Card Number＿＿＿＿＿＿＿＿＿＿＿＿＿＿ Exp. Date＿＿＿＿＿

Signature＿＿＿＿＿＿＿＿＿＿＿＿＿＿＿＿＿＿＿

Telephone＿＿＿＿＿＿＿ FAX＿＿＿＿＿＿＿＿＿＿

Name＿＿＿＿＿＿＿＿＿＿＿＿＿＿＿＿＿＿＿＿

Organization＿＿＿＿＿＿＿＿＿＿＿＿＿＿＿＿

Street＿＿＿＿＿＿＿＿＿＿＿＿＿＿＿＿＿＿＿＿

City＿＿＿＿＿＿＿＿＿ State/Zip＿＿＿＿＿＿＿＿

Country＿＿＿＿＿＿＿＿ ☐ Home Address ☐ Organization Address

Please Reference Telephone Order Code 132A

Harvard Business School Publications